BOYHOOD MEMORIES OF A CARIBOO TOWN

LILLOOET STORIES

GORDON E. WHITNEY

COPYRIGHT

Gordon E. Whitney

Boyhood Memories of a Cariboo Town

Lillooet Stories

COVER ARTWORK & GAMES ILLUSTRATION by Kathy Whitney

ALL OTHER ARTWORK by Gordon Whitney

COVER DESIGN & INTERIOR LAYOUT by Stephanie Candiago

CONTENTS

for my children

DISCLAIMER

This is a work of creative nonfiction. I've portrayed the happenings of my youth in Lillooet to the best of my memory. In some cases I have compressed events; in others I have left out minor details. Any embellishments are for the purpose of telling a good story.

INTRODUCTION BY LAUREL WHITNEY

Since as early as I can remember, our family has made an annual pilgrimage to my dad's hometown of Lillooet, BC. The moment school was out in June, we four kids would squeeze into the back seat of our family car, which our mom had already packed full of camping supplies. Starting from south Burnaby, where my dad had proudly built our beautiful family home, we would cross the farmlands of the Fraser Valley, turn abruptly left at Hope, and begin the long journey up the Fraser Canyon.

The landscape was imposing yet strikingly beautiful. As our car climbed each hill of the canyon, Dad would entertain us with lessons in geology and geography, tales of BC's Gold Rush and the PGE railroad, and his childhood memories of surviving the Depression in Lillooet. Along the way, he would point out remnants of the Cariboo Wagon Road and keep us riveted with stories about his childhood hero, Tom Manson; his youthful encounters with the unemployed men who rode the rails; and his many boyhood fishing escapades.

Dad was born in Lillooet in 1925, in a rented second-storey flat above a store on Main Street. When the Great Depression hit, he was not yet old enough to be in school.

Even though his father, Reuben, was a talented carpenter, the family subsisted on monthly government payments of thirty dollars "relief." Dad's mom, Nina, was only fourteen when she married, and she always struggled with her health. She lost several babies in childbirth. When Ernie, her first-born, was nine years old, he went to live with his grandparents on a small farm on the flats beside the town of Lillooet. Ernie did chores for his grandparents, and I guess it was one less mouth to feed for Nina. My father's sister Deilla, when she was old enough, was also sent to live away, although she lived with relatives in Vancouver. Since Reuben did not own any property, the rest of the family—which included Gordon (my dad) and his other two brothers Allan and Doug—lived in a series of rented homes. After the Main Street home, they moved to the community of Gold Bridge for a brief period. Next, they moved back to Lillooet, into another rented home belonging to a Mr. Wo Hing. Eventually, the family settled in a shack Reuben built on the rocky shores of the Cayoosh Creek next to town. Truth be told, they were squatters, but Dad recalls this period as the happiest of his childhood.

Dad started school early, at the age of five, and he excelled. His teachers skipped him ahead by an additional two grades. But my dad's reputation as a top scholar was bittersweet; it won him both admiration and resentment. He spent many a pleasant afternoon around the table at the Jim residence, helping their five children with homework and joining them for supper. Mr. Jim, a refugee from China, treated my dad like one of his own. But the pioneer families of Lillooet resented young Gordon Whitney. These farmers and ranchers were the local elite. To them, Gordon was "white trash," only marginally better than the "Indians" who lived on the reserve beside the town.

In 1939, World War II broke out, ending the Depression and triggering a sudden shortage of workers. My dad's father landed a job in New Westminster, and the family left Lillooet for good.

Dad graduated from high school in New Westminster at the tender age of sixteen and started his studies at the University of British Columbia. He eventually had a long, successful career as a teacher in Vancouver. We knew he was well-loved by his students because so many of them visited him at our home. Dad often returned from school laden with gifts from their parents, such as bottles of homemade Italian wine. But his emotional attachment to Lillooet remained firmly implanted, and we, his children, know this better than anyone else. When we were small, while Mom was busy studying on the weekends to finish her bachelor's degree, Dad would gather us up in the car. He would drive us to Stanley Park or the North Shore mountains, where he taught us bushwhacking skills and, of course, how to fish for trout. I can remember wading into the cold waters of Lynn Creek beside him and marvelling at his geological knowledge as he pulled up one glistening rock specimen after another for us to examine. Our childhood was filled with such impromptu lessons. The outdoors was Dad's favourite classroom, and I am sure these weekend excursions were his way of reliving his childhood in Lillooet.

When I had children, I, too, took them to Lillooet. We were always accompanied by my dad, whose tour of the town included the site of the wartime Japanese internment camp, the piles of rocks where the Chinese miners had sluiced for gold, the shores of the Fraser River where the First Nations people dried their salmon, and the home of Joe Pizzi. We would listen in awe as he explained how, as a boy, he soothed his hunger by stealing the fruit from Joe's trees or by trading fish for doughnuts with the local hobos.

Our childhood was greatly enriched by his tales of Lillooet, but I was completely taken by surprise when Dad decided to write down his memories shortly after his ninety-second birthday. It was a treat to receive emails from him every week with stories attached. It's the tenth decade of his life, yet he is as prolific a writer today as he was when he first attended university more than seventy-five years ago. The stories contained in this book are his memoirs. It gives me great pleasure to be able to share them with you.

Wo Hing House, Gordon's family's second Lillooet home.

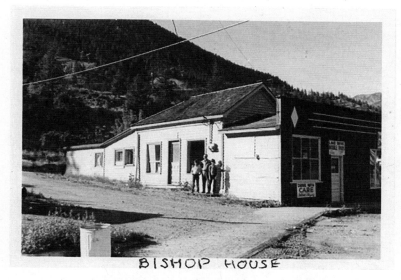

Bishop House where Gordon was born.

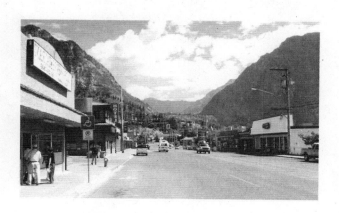

Lillooet's Main Street, looking west.

View from upper town flat.

Gordon and his son-in-law, Napo, looking north from the west
bank of the Fraser River.

ONE
BACK TO LILLOOET

To get by automobile from Vancouver to the village of Lillooet in the Cariboo—two-hundred-odd miles away—you have a choice of three routes: (1) drive from Vancouver to Lytton, head east to Ashcroft, drive north through Cache Creek, continue onto Pavilion Lake, turn west, and drop down to Lillooet, situated on the west bank of the Fraser River; (2) drive from Vancouver to Lytton and continue forty-seven miles north along the Fraser to the village of Lillooet; (3) drive north on the beautiful Sea-to-Sky Highway to Squamish and head east from Squamish to Pemberton. From there, climb up the eastern switchback side of Pemberton Valley onto the picturesque Duffy Lake Road, which will lead you to Lillooet.

I have always chosen the route via the Sea-to-Sky Highway for its scenic beauty. Driving north from Vancouver, with Howe Sound on your left and the Coast Mountains on your right, the scenery is not unlike that of Scandinavia with its many fjords. It is a sheer pleasure to behold. I choose the word *sheer* because it aptly describes the topography; the Sea-to-Sky Highway has been carved—blasted—out of one hundred miles of a granitic mountainside.

In the Hungry Thirties of the Great Depression, there was

no highway connecting Vancouver to Squamish, nor was there a railway. You had to travel on a Union steamship from Vancouver to Squamish. Nowadays you can travel by car in less than two hours.

When my family finally left Lillooet for Vancouver in 1939, we rode south to Squamish on the PGE: the Pacific Great Eastern Railway, or, as the locals called it, the "Please Go Easy Railway"—a commentary on its slow rate of travel. At Squamish, we boarded a Union steamship. I remember with great pleasure that on the upper deck of that steamship, we were once serenaded by a pair of wonderful musicians, a violinist and an accordionist, Swedish miners on holiday from the Bralorne mine near Lillooet. The two men played dance music, waltzes, and two-steps all the way to Vancouver, the music echoing wonderfully across the water from the steep mountainsides of the fjords. I imagined that the two musicians were dreaming of their homeland, Sweden, as they played.

These days, after taking the Sea-to-Sky to Squamish, you must drive eastward up a long valley to Pemberton. (On our return trip to Lillooet, we usually stop for lunch at McDonalds.) After lunch you must ascend several hundred feet on a steep twisting switchback road up the east side of the Pemberton Valley. At the top, you will find yourself in alpine country, at the west end of the Duffy Lake Road to Lillooet.

Stop for a few minutes, get out of your car, and scan the scenery. To the northwest you will see the Mount Meager glacier, which blankets the Mount Meager volcano. The volcano, according to seismologists, is soon about to erupt. Do you remember Mount St. Helen's, which erupted in Washington State forty years ago? The seismologists, having monitored Mount Meager for several years, have recently discovered new fumaroles belching sulphur dioxide and methane. This opening of fumaroles indicates major movements inside the volcano. An eruption will cause landslides, block the Pemberton Valley, dam the Pemberton

River, and flood the town itself. They think Whistler may also be affected. Whistler and Pemberton, beware!

After you have looked at the Meager ice field and put the predicted eruption out of mind, drive on toward Lillooet, park at the nearest picnic site, lay out some food on one of the picnic tables, and wait for a visit from the resident family of beggars. These are our beautiful, brazen Canada jays, cousins of our Blue Jays but dressed in their own distinctive grey and white plumage. The locals have renamed them whisky jacks and "camp robbers." I always enjoyed their tactic of accepting my offerings off the table (and sometimes off my hand), quickly flying away to wedge the morsels in amongst the sharp needles of a nearby spruce tree, and returning for numerous refills. They are quite polite compared to the pigeons, crows, and seagulls of Vancouver. A Stanley Park seagull will steal your fish and chips off your table while you are eating, almost right out of your mouth.

Later, as you head east along the Duffy Lake Road toward Lillooet, you will pass on your right a large glacier with ample snow fields: a perfect place for a ski resort. And you will pass numerous creeks like Joffre Creek and Phair Creek, which drain the runoff from the ice field above and empty into Duffy Lake immediately below the roadway on your left. As you proceed eastward, you cannot see that you are perched high on the side of a wide valley hidden from view by dense forest: the Anderson Lake / Seton Lake Valley. Duffy Lake perches on the mountainside on your immediate left and empties, several miles further on, into the headwaters of Cayoosh Creek. The Cayoosh, in turn, empties downstream into the Fraser River at Lillooet.

Follow the Duffy Lake road for twenty-five miles and descend down the steep Cayoosh Creek canyon, where the village of Lillooet sits on a glacial bench on the west bank of the Fraser River, two thousand feet below.

Lillooet also lies at the eastern end of a long east-west chain of lakes: Anderson Lake on the west and its partner, Seton Lake, on the east, which empties into the west bank of the Fraser River. In the Lill'wat Indian language, Lillooet means "where five waters meet," namely Bridge River, Town Creek, Seton Creek, Cayoosh Creek, and the mighty Fraser.

The town of Lillooet sits on real soil that is rich and arable. It was the original site chosen by the settlers, miners, and merchants who came up from California around 1860 after their own gold rush on the Sacramento River petered out.

Lillooet, a snug little town—or village, as some call it today—sits on the west bank of the Fraser River, facing south toward Lytton, forty-seven miles downriver. The town occupies one of the many remnants of the ten-thousand-year-old glacial lake beds that were placer-mined from 1849 until the gold ran out, some as late as 1937.

When I was a child, the Lillooet residents proudly called themselves Lillooet pioneers, and newcomers had to be careful not to offend these established snobs, or else they would suffer the consequences.

Some of the original families moved into town from hay and cattle ranches poised on the nearby flats up and down both sides of the Fraser River. They more or less ran the town. We Whitneys were part of the poor class. My family lived in poor housing in a state of poverty, subsisting on welfare most of the time. Welfare, in Lillooet, was called "relief"—and being on relief was a social stigma!

I was born in the latter part of December. My mother used to say I was an Easter egg that became, after nine months in the womb, a Christmas present. My mother swore that I was born three days before Christmas on December 22, 1925. Yet my birth certificate lists the date as December 20. My illiterate grandmother, who went to the Lillooet courthouse to register my birth, was likely the cause of this discrepancy. According to my mother, she chose the wrong day. Anyway, my birth date, in my opinion, resulted in my mother prematurely registering me for Grade 1 in Lillooet Elementary School at the age of five years and nine months, perhaps to get me out from under her feet at home. She should have waited until September 1931, my optimal sixth year, giving my body more time to grow in stature and my mind more time to develop socially.

I should have also, perhaps, spent a year in a kindergarten, but, alas, no such institution existed in Lillooet. I was a small child, a runt, but exceptionally bright—and for that reason, I was despised instead of admired by many of my classmates and their parents. I now think some parents felt that a small, poorly dressed boy on welfare had no business being persistently the top-ranking student.

I suffered bullying in the early grades and much derision and envy from my male classmates. In later grades, I suffered social rejection by my female classmates. I never felt physically capable of fighting back, so I suffered in silence and became docile.

My saving grace was that I fell in love with school. I loved the teacher and her beautiful clothing. I loved being near books, pens, pencils, paper, blackboards, white and coloured chalk, blackboard brushes. I even enjoyed my chores for the teacher, such as banging brushes together in the courtyard to knock the chalk dust out of them. I still am in love with school. That love was undoubtedly why I became a teacher. I think I was born to be a teacher.

In my memory, the impoverished Lillooet rented houses I lived in couldn't really be called homes. There were no children's books for me to read or musical instruments on which to take lessons. To make matters worse, I was born with painful astigmatic eyesight that was never tested or diagnosed until I entered high school at age fourteen in New Westminster. I remember the nurse there commenting that she couldn't understand how I had managed to excel academically all those years with such a visual handicap.

So I was unfortunately born into a culturally barren household, to ignorant, unschooled parents whose only interest, in retrospect, was enlarging the number of children in our family. Our house was, to me, only a place to eat and sleep. And since Lillooet possessed no public library and we had no radio to induce me to stay home in the evenings, I spent much of my time roaming the streets with a pal or two and observing the daylight and twilight activities of the townspeople, about whom I am now writing in these short stories.

In September 1939, I started Grade 10 at the Duke of Connaught High School, an upper-class secondary school in New Westminster. I was the only poor white student in my class—all the other students belonged to elite families near the area of Queen's Park. By the end of June 1942, I had completed senior matric, equivalent to first-year university. Since I was never counselled at home or in school, I blindly followed several of my classmates into UBC's School of Applied Science. That was a mistake that could have been avoided.

However, in 1947, I graduated with a bachelor of science degree in geological engineering and immediately got a job in the Alberta oil fields. I worked for three years for an American oil company but became completely disenchanted with my profession as an oil geologist. So I returned to New Westminster in 1950 and, with money I had saved, attended the Provincial Normal School in Vancouver. I graduated in 1951 with honours and was hired by the Vancouver School Board as a high school mathematics teacher.

For thirty-five happy years, I taught mathematics and sponsored a poetry club at Gladstone Secondary School. I retired in 1985 at the age of sixty and immediately enrolled in art school, spending 1986 and 1987, the first two years of retirement, in the Fine Arts Department of Langara College in

Vancouver. It was a delightful, life-changing experience. I won scholarships, but most important, I developed great skills in drawing and painting.

Now in my ninety-fourth year, I am exploring the field of literature, writing poetry and a series of short stories that comprise a sort of autobiography of the first thirteen years of my life. These years I spent in my former hometown of Lillooet, a one-horse town in the Cariboo.

I do occasionally revisit the town, often visiting the museum to gaze on the portrait of the dear friend and mentor of my youth, Tom Manson. It is an enlargement of a photograph I took years ago as he stood in the doorway of his niece's (Hilda Haylmore's) home on Main Street. This large black-and-white portrait now hangs permanently on the museum's wall. Tom Manson was a father-figure to me. His family were some of the first pioneers to settle in the Lillooet area, more than half a century before I was born. I learned that he and his father had worked as guides for the big game hunters who came from the USA and Europe, and that he was one of the boys from Lillooet who had fought in World War One. By the time my family arrived in Lillooet, Tom was already semi-retired, and he and his mother lived on an orchard right next to the town. I would say hello to him whenever I passed his place. Tom always took the time to talk to me, and some of my most memorable afternoons were spent accompanying him as he strolled along Main Street. Tom was my source of knowledge about Lillooet and about its colourful citizens. He also knew a great deal about the Indigenous people who lived next door on the reserve. Tom never tired of answering my questions; despite our large difference in age, we obviously enjoyed each other's company. And I have to credit him for schooling me in the fine art of trout fishing; it was my favourite form of entertainment and my main source of protein as a boy.

Tom lived a long life and he finally passed away when he

was in his mid-nineties. My family left Lillooet when I was thirteen, but I have returned there to visit many times. My favourite time of year is June when the saskatoon berries are ripe. The local Indigenous name for them is *tsaqwem*. And sometimes in July I can still find wild chokecherries that cause your lips to pucker in response to their fierce, wild acidity. With luck, I may find a bush of soopollalie berries—local name *hoo'sh'um*—which our mother used to eggbeater-whip into a fresh meringue. The generous addition of white sugar made this a delicious treat we called "Siwash ice cream."

And, of course, I eventually head for the cemetery, reread the grave directory, gaze on the names on the gravestones of old and young friends, and recall happier, nostalgic, and even very sad days from that portion of my life, 1925 to 1939, in the old pioneer gold rush town of Lillooet.

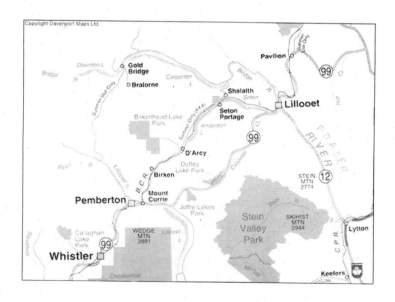

Military engineer's drawing of Lillooet and Mount
Brew, 1860.

1860: Lillooet, "mile zero" of the Gold Rush Trail.

Descending the Cayoosh Creek canyon.

Jack Pine forest.

Duffy Lake Road viewpoint, Cayoosh canyon below.

Fountain Ridge, east Lillooet.

West bank viewpoint near Texas Creek Road.

Spear grass meadow south of Lillooet.

TWO
A CHILD'S WINTER IN LILLOOET

During the Hungry Thirties, the winter climate in Lillooet was much more severe than it is today. I can remember the temperature dropping to minus thirty degrees Fahrenheit. We referred to it as "thirty below." There were many days when the north wind blew fiercely down the Fraser River and through Lillooet, making my daily walk to school a real torture. I had to turn my back to the wind whenever possible.

School was a welcome haven, always well heated by means of a horizontal, oversized cylindrical stove that could take a four-foot-long chunk of fir or pine. Our cloakroom was also our entrance hall, with a row of coat hooks on the wall that held our toques, scarves, and heavy winter coats above the rows of snow-clogged winter rubber boots, which we called gum rubbers.

So our large schoolroom was a nice place to be, especially if your desk was close to the stove. Some of the older boys, like my favourite, John Wing, carried firewood in from the woodshed behind the school.

Winter clothing for our family was mostly homemade. Mine were knitted items: sweater, cap, scarf, mitts, and socks. After all, who could afford to buy "store-bought" clothing in those tough times? The Whitney family, on welfare, couldn't. Some winters I did sport a jacket made of melton cloth, ordered from the T. Eaton Co. in Winnipeg. But it wasn't really new. It was a hand-me-down from my older brother Allan. Winter coats were big items that could not be knitted and thus were never thrown away. They were mended, patched, darned, and handed down to younger siblings. More important for temperature control were the hand-knitted sweaters worn under the coats.

Winter underwear, especially for boys, consisted of one-piece long johns, Stanfield's, with a front that buttoned down to the waist and a two-buttoned flap in the rear for obvious reasons. I think girls wore a female version. Going to the john, the biffy, answering nature's call, or "leaving the room" involved making a cold dash to the outhouse, latching the door to ensure privacy, and dropping down bodily onto a frigid wooden toilet seat. That was an unforgettable experience, like an aeroplane coming in for a three-point landing with the flaps down but making a really bad two-pointer instead.

I remember cold fingers and cold toes. My boots were always gum rubbers or high-top gumboots with blue felt insoles which, at the end of the day, were always soaking wet and had to be removed at home and dried out near the heater to be ready for the next day. What a treat that was, to remove soaking-wet boots and insoles and toast blue-stained tootsies near the stove, sometimes on the open oven door.

You could never keep snow from getting into the tops of gum rubbers, even by pulling wool socks up over the bottoms of pant legs. School recesses were spent on the snow-covered playing field, so our boots never had a chance to dry out until we got home from school.

Woollen mitts were also a necessity. Making and throwing snowballs was great fun, but it meant sodden mittens when we were back inside the classroom.

There were more exotic winter activities, of course. My

older brother Allan and his friends skied. I don't remember whether or not he made his own skies, but I once tried to make myself a pair. They worked fine, but the ski harness was beyond my skills, and the skis proved a failure.

But some of us got together and made bobsleds long enough for six passengers to toboggan down Bouvette's Hill and the Rancherie Hill near the PGE Railway station. Allan and his friends Harry Webster and Murray Downton also used to hunt grouse and snowshoe rabbits on the East Lillooet flats in winter.

We boys made our own toys. All of us were keen on making tools, toys, and weapons so we could play games such as Cowboys and Indians and Cops and Robbers. Once, out of necessity, I even made a pair of stout, canvas-and-sheepskin-lined mittens. Mr. Jim Larter—the blacksmith, gas station owner, and morgue custodian—was the father of two of my playmates, the twins Peter and Paul Larter. These two adventuresome, mischief-seeking boys gave me and our friends access to a wonderful supply of adult tools. This was big-time stuff, and I suppose there was danger therein, but none of us boys ever got hurt using the tools. And I really enjoyed helping Mr. Larter at his forge on cold winter Saturday mornings, pumping the bellows for him while he fashioned and fitted horseshoes onto real live horses. We were allowed to make horseshoe nails into finger rings on the anvil. Mr. Larter's blacksmith shop was where I made my skis and helped my friends make our bobsled.

Life in winter was exhilarating, though bitingly cold at times, especially at bedtime and during the night. It was a sharp contrast to our modern times, with its thermal clothing and central heating but also its limited access to out-of-doors play areas.

Fun in the snow was always available, and even though I loved school, I was never too unhappy when school had to be closed after a heavy snowfall. We children loved to play in the

snow, sleigh ride, snow fight, and slide down the icy "Dips,"
the two gullies adjacent to the school playgrounds and within
easy walking distance from our home. When I was seven and
eight years old we lived in a house rented from a Mr. Wo Hing,
which was located in the alley behind Blanche Vinal's house.
Our winter activities were wild, great fun, but the freedom and
abandon sometimes led to accidents, large and small.

Snowballing was fun, but it had its dangers. In Grade 1, I
was struck in the eye when I rounded a corner during recess
and walked into a soaker—a deliberately wetted snowball—
meant for someone else. Sixty years later, I had to have a
cataract removed from that eye and a plastic lens implanted.

Accompanying innocent mischief like this were dirtier
deeds, like the one that took place on a cold snowy November
evening in Lillooet, with two feet of snow on the ground and
more still falling. Main Street was, I grant, poorly lit, and the
sidewalks were only cleared enough to allow two persons to
pass. Deep snow was piled along the edges where the sidewalk
joined the street. Pedestrian traffic was minimal, but
occasionally people braved the snow and the cold to go about
their business.

Children, however, had great fun building giant snowmen
in their front yards. The November snow was easily packed to
a high degree of compactness. On this evening, a group of four
boys busied themselves creating a large snowball, chest high,
on the curb down on Main Street, right outside the doorway of
the See Hing Lung grocery store. Mr. See Hing Lung was an
aged, respected merchant who, along with his son Louie,
owned and operated a grocery store, restaurant, and rooming
house on Main Street.

Passersby paid no attention to the boys, who quickly built
their large snowball from snow that had been shovelled off the
sidewalk and dumped, more than two feet high, onto the edge
of the street.

At the right moment, when no pedestrians or cars were

visible, one of the boys waited quietly at the store's doorway while the others gently pushed the snowball up beside him. Then, in a flash, he pushed open the door and jumped aside. The other three thrust the snowball through the doorway into the store. In one last, deft move, the first boy gave the snowball a final vigorous shove, forcing it into the store and up against the hot cast-iron stove that warmed the entrance. Then, quickly shutting the door behind him, he and the other boys ran off and hid from view.

The customers and clerks in the store, faced with such a catastrophe, were left gasping in shock. The store owner, Mr. See Hing Lung, Sr., stared helplessly at the cloud of steam rising from the stove and the meltwater pooling on the floor and flowing rapidly toward the back of the store.

The Caucasian perpetrators of this crime sneaked away into the back alley behind Jim Larter's blacksmith shop and crept homeward, smiling with smug satisfaction. The next day they bragged about their accomplishment to friends, and soon the whole town knew about it.

There was no punishment, verbal or physical, meted out to the boys. In fact, as I walked along Main Street in the days following and passed in front of the beer parlour and Billy Taverna's barbershop, I heard many adults chuckling over the incident as they retold the story, relishing the torment inflicted on the old Chinese storekeeper.

Much worse than any local boys' mean-spirited antics, however, were the occasional tragedies borne of the unpredictable wildness of everyday life at that time. Four dried-up town creek beds had, over the years, dissected the flats on which the town had been built. The creek had changed its direction for unknown reasons, possibly from human interference, but it no longer flowed through the town because it had been dammed near the base of the mountain to form the reservoir, our town's fresh water supply. One branch of the creek had flowed in a wooden flume behind the Vinal family home; another had flowed through Joe Russell's field right past his house on Main Street; another had flowed past George Prosser's house on Main Street; and a fourth went underground through Tommy Hurley's side yard. Of course, these gullies were all filled in as the town grew, and Main Street now passes over all four.

These dried-up gullies became our wintertime sliding slopes: our "Dips," as we called them. Big Dip and Little Dip were both located near the site of the town's present-day public library. We iced these slopes to the desired degree of slipperiness by carrying pails of water from Mr. Hurley's basement tap or an indoor tap in the school and pouring the water on the snow-packed slopes. We made primitive luges from cardboard boxes, flattened or un-flattened, and some of the older boys even went down the slopes on ice skates.

The first sliders to arrive at the site after school or after supper would build a bonfire, using wood and scraps of paper brought from home. We all brought spuds to roast in the fire. It was a real pioneer pleasure to break open those blackened nuggets and fill our mouths with hot, fluffy, cooked potato starch. And the fire was necessary to warm us up, so we could go on sliding until it was time to go home.

Safety was always on our minds, and the Dips were safe from automobile traffic — such as there was in back alleys and on Main Street — but, boys being boys, we didn't always take our parents' warnings seriously.

One winter, several of us decided to ride our sleds down Eagan's Alley, across Main Street, and past Larter's Garage (now the Esso Station). If we were lucky, we'd slide across the PGE railroad tracks and down the steep, winding road to Mrs. Foster's farm. (This farm no longer exists, having been used up for housing lots.)

Sledding down Eagan's Alley was a very dangerous activity that necessitated having one boy stand as lookout at the junction of Eagan's Alley and Main Street. This was okay during daylight hours, when a lookout could wave and warn of oncoming cars, but at night it became hazardous. To avoid accidents, we used two flashlights, one with red crepe paper covering the lens and the other with green. We would rush to the alley right after school and continue sledding until dark.

On one such evening, around five o'clock, we curtailed our sledding and our ranks thinned as mothers called children home to supper. Bobby Hurley left, Clifford Jim left, and the Larter twins left. Georgie Hurley, who lived right on the alley, had gone inside, and Boyo Hurley and I were the only two left. I could hear my mother calling me. (At that time we lived close to the alley in a rented house across from Blanche Vinal's present home.) I was holding the flashlights because at the moment, I was the lookout.

Boyo had just come back from a successful slide, towing his sled behind him, having made it down Eagan's Alley, past Larter's Garage, and down past Blanche Vinal's place. But it was suppertime, and, besides, it had started to snow again, quite heavily. I told Boyo we had to quit for the night. I reminded him that his kid brother, Bobby, had gone home, and that he was supposed to go home too. I remember him saying, "Okay," as I headed for home, ducking my head against the falling snow and taking the two flashlights with me.

A short time later, as I was getting ready to sit down to supper, there was a knock on our door, and a breathless voice said that there had been an accident. Boyo Hurley, sledding down Eagan's Alley, had ridden into the right front wheel of Bill Arthur's car as Bill headed westward up Main Street.

The news drew us all away from our dinners, and soon a crowd of shocked onlookers had gathered in front of Doc Stewart's house on Main Street. Boyo, unconscious, was being placed into the rumble seat of Ma Murray's red roadster. He was taken to the Lytton Hospital, where Dr. Ellis examined him and sent him on to Vancouver.

Boyo died a week later, in the Vancouver General Hospital, of severe head injuries. He had never regained consciousness.

Needless to say, that put an end to sledding down Eagan's Alley and sadly took one of our cherished companions away from his family. We were in shock for days, and none more so than poor Mr. Arthur, who was, of course, blameless. I remember thinking that Boyo—his real name was Tommy—was the image of his father, Tommy Hurley, Sr. Boyo's death must have broken his father's heart.

Now when I look at the old school photos and see Boyo standing with his classmates, it all comes back to me. I remember with heavy heart that terrible accident, and that grey winter day when our whole school attended Boyo's funeral to watch his coffin being lowered into the frozen ground.

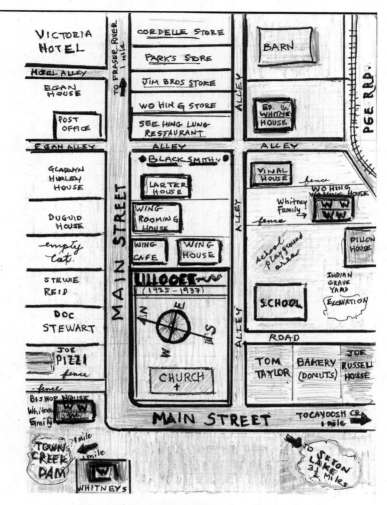

1930s Main Street neighbourhood, drawn from memory.

Eight - year - old Gordon with Nina, his mother in front of the primary grades schoolhouse.

THREE
GOLD BRIDGE, 1931–32

The first house I lived in — and in fact, the house I was born in — was a house my father rented from a Mr. Fred Bishop for eight dollars a month. The house is still sitting there on Main Street, right where the cairn stands on the sidewalk, announcing that Lillooet was mile zero for the wagon trains heading north to the gold fields. Can you imagine renting a house for that amount of money? I think the average wage for a labourer must have been one dollar a day. Eight dollars was big money.

When I was two years old, Mr. Bishop, I was told, was postmaster of a place called Moha, located somewhere northwest of Lillooet. I always wanted to know where Moha was, but nobody seemed to know. "You get to it," they said, "if you follow the unpaved road westward along the Bridge River road and turn off at Yalakom Creek." The Bridge River flows out of the Coast Range Mountains, eastward down the wide Bridge River Valley, and enters the Fraser River at a point three miles north of Lillooet. I can remember that Moha was in gold mining country, near the Minto, Bralorne, and Pioneer mines. I don't think it was even a village, just a post office for the ranchers in that area.

Anyway, Fred Bishop used to drive his truck down this narrow Bridge River road to Lillooet once a month to pick up the mail for Moha at the Lillooet post office. My father had made a strange deal with him: on the last day of the month, Mr. Bishop was allowed to stay overnight in our kitchen and sleep on a folding cot that my father set up for him. He came on schedule, stayed overnight, got up the next morning around five o'clock, and cooked himself a breakfast of pork sausages, fried eggs, bread fried in pork fat, and coffee. He used our kitchen utensils, fry pan, dishes, cutlery, coffee pot, and a cup. He left the dirty dishes for my mother to clean and put away.

He also always left a few cooked pork sausages in the frying pan. I don't know why he didn't buy just the right amount of sausages. Maybe they came in a certain sized package. After Mr. Bishop had departed for Moha in his truck, carrying off the mail that had been stowed for him in several sealed canvas post-office bags, these delicacies were eaten by whichever member of our family got to the kitchen first.

I vaguely remember him as a stout, elderly man, red-faced, wearing dark pants supported by wide suspenders that stretched over a grey shirt. He always wore an old battered cowboy hat, a Stetson that had seen better days. My memory of him was vague, but I had vivid memories of his pork sausages. I think I was able, most mornings, to be the first up after he left and win the prize of those leftovers.

I still fancy the flavour of smoked breakfast sausage.

My family stayed in the Bishop house until I was six years old. Then, in the summer of 1931, my father got work with the Department of Public Works as a grader man in summer and a snowplow operator in winter. So we moved from the rented Bishop house in Lillooet to another residence: two tent houses in the small village of Gold Bridge. Gold Bridge was located twenty-five miles upstream from the mouth of the Fraser on the south bank of the Bridge River and on the road to the Bralorne and Pioneer mines, which were located high up on the mountainside. The tent houses were located on the Bridge River flats below the town of Gold Bridge. I remember they were rented from a Mr. Henseller.

That was a wonderful summer. Some friendly local boys took my brothers and me upstream to a large open gravel bar, where we used heaving lines baited with chunks of fresh pork to catch sixteen- and eighteen-inch steelhead trout. The fish were heading upstream to spawn in Little Gun Lake. Spawning fish usually aren't hungry, but these were definitely so.

I would never have dreamed of using fresh pork for steelhead trout, but it worked. I had used grasshoppers and earthworms for rainbow trout, or salmon eggs for Dolly Varden bait when the salmon were spawning in Cayoosh Creek back down in Lillooet.

Summer passed agreeably. My two older brothers, Ernest and Allan, found new girlfriends, but I was without new playmates until I started school in September. I was at that time six and a half years old, my next birthday coming up at Christmastime.

Our school was a one-room school, with classes ranging from Grade 4 to Grade 9. My brother Allan was in Grade 9, but Ernest was taking Grade 11 by correspondence at home in the tent house. I was entered into Grade 4 in the one-room Gold Bridge school, along with another boy.

Snow began to fall in November, and living in tent houses became awkward, so we moved. The main reason for our move was, I am sure, my two older brothers. They were living in their separate tent house, and one evening they had a heated argument, which ended with one brother urinating on their small wood-burning heater. The stench of burning urine was awful.

My brothers couldn't stand it, I guess, so they both had to move into our big tent house. I knew what burnt urine smelled like: really rotten! Yech, I never want to encounter that odour ever again.

Anyway, the upshot of my two brothers' stupid argument was that our parents decided to move uptown into a rented house near the school. I was glad. Walking to school a mile uphill, often at twenty below zero, was not only terribly tough going but could also be dangerous. One could have an accident and freeze to death.

Our teacher was Miss Harris, a pretty blonde young woman. I think she was of Welsh extraction because every morning, my classmate and I were asked to sing "Men of Harlech," which she referred to as the Welsh national anthem. I wonder now if the students in the higher grades didn't come to hate us two boy sopranos. I loved the song and still do. Sometimes, I sit in my apartment and accompany myself on my ukulele, singing "Men of Harlech," reminiscing, and fondly remembering Miss Harris.

I recall the time I found a piece of paper on the frozen snow, outside the school on my way home. I bent down and could see my teacher's name on it, so I cut the hard snow around the piece of paper gently with my jackknife and carried it carefully home, down on the flats, and placed it on a plate on the kitchen table to thaw. Then I put it very carefully on a clean tea towel and let it dry out. Holy moly, it was a cheque made out to my teacher, Miss Harris, for the sum of one hundred dollars. I think that it was her monthly paycheque from the Bridge River school board.

I showed it to my mother, who put it carefully into a clean envelope and took it to my teacher the next day at noon. Miss Harris never said anything to me, but she smiled a lot at me in class from then on. I think she was embarrassed at losing her cheque. I was in love with her, so I forgave her for not thanking me.

There was only a kitchen range to heat the newly rented house, so my father bought two electric hot plates for our two bedrooms. I think now that we were fortunate to have escaped our house going up in flames, because we put the hot plates under our beds.

But because our new house was only two blocks from school, I didn't have to head home right after school was out. I managed to meet a new friend from Grade 5, Peter Chiz. Peter and I wandered around the town together. We didn't have skis or sleds, but we found a small slope near our two houses, made some cardboard sliding mats from discarded boxes, and spent many happy hours at that sport, sliding downhill with our feet tucked into the curved front edges of our mats and climbing back up to the top of our slippery slide. That was hard work, but well worth the effort. The joy of sliding is fresh in my memory after all these years.

One other friend—or should I just say "friend?"—almost got me into trouble with the authorities. Our so-called friendship was short-lived. One Saturday morning we went around the back alleys, collecting empty beer bottles to take to Mr. Arthur's corner store. We could get fifteen cents a dozen. That was the price of three Oh Henry! candy bars—well worth the effort.

The routine was for Mr. Arthur to first examine the bottles and then take them down to his storage room in the basement of his store before he paid us. I guess he had no other place to store them, and as soon as his head disappeared down the stairs, my "friend" loaded up his pockets with low-profile chocolate bars. Finally, Mr. Arthur reappeared and paid us each fifteen cents. The next time he asked me to go beer bottle collecting, I made sure I had an excuse not to. I could always talk my mother out of a dime for candy. Poor, innocent, gullible Mr. Arthur!

My brother Allan was a go-getter, and he was also looking to make some cash. He ended his job hunt with a dandy, well-paying offer, a deal to split firewood for the madam of the local house of ill repute—in other words, the whorehouse. I think he got two dollars, twice a week. That's four dollars a week for splitting firewood and kindling. He said the madam paid him well, because back in Lillooet, he had gotten one dollar a day for sweeping out two classrooms, and the job was dirty and time consuming. But two dollars was two dollars. Allan preferred splitting wood for the madam because it was clean work and fast. He was a whiz at wood splitting. You should have seen him. Man, he was fast, and it took only an hour each time. I thought it was a good deal, but I really didn't know anything about odd jobs or the pay scale. He did get a lot of teasing from his older brother Ernest, however, about being paid "in kind."

At that time I didn't know what the joking was all about. Allan won the argument by saying to Ernest, "You're just jealous."

"Hah," said Ernest. "Jealous? Of getting paid to split wood? When I get to Vancouver next summer, I'll be making real money." And he did just that. In two years, he was apprenticed to become a millwright, and five years after that, he had his own business manufacturing handles for all kinds of hand tools.

I didn't know until many years later that one of the residents of Gold Bridge was the grandfather of Bobby Hurley, my school mate and fishing buddy in Lillooet. Bobby's grandfather, Mr. Charlie Owens, knew all about Allan cutting firewood for the madam and her girls, because the whorehouse was near the bunkhouse in which he lived. (I think Mr. Owens may even have been a client.) He had spotted Allan working on the madam's woodpile every so often. "He's a fine-looking young lad," Mr. Owens remarked, "but he'd better be careful around those women." He must have been joking, because he had a big grin on his face. "How old is Allan anyway?" Mr. Owens went on.

"He's fifteen, Charlie," my father replied, "but you don't have to worry about him. He's chasing after a girl his own age, a girl in his class in school. She's a looker. Her name is Joan Bergeven, I believe."

"Well, I'd best be off and get on home. My wife will be worrying by now. She worries.

Here, Reuben," Charlie Owens said, handing my father a brown bag with six pancakes inside. "Leftovers from breakfast. Take them home with you. I always cook too many, and any time you pass by, you can take them home."

I remember Charlie Owens's fluffy pancakes. They had eggs in them and tasted to me like cake. I always ate my share. I was always happy to come in contact with food. We usually had porridge for breakfast. Not that I didn't like porridge topped off with Pacific condensed milk and water, plus a heaping tablespoon of brown sugar. Still, multigrain porridge for breakfast, along with toast and jam and coffee, didn't hold a candle to Mr. Charlie Owens's pancakes.

Years later, during one of my long summer holidays back in Lillooet from Burnaby, Charlie Owens's name came up in a conversation with Tom Manson. From the time I was a boy, I had a father figure in Tom. He was an accomplished cowboy — a real cowboy — and he was also very skilled at fishing. He lived on his property in Lillooet with his elderly mother. (I believe he was unmarried and had no children.) Tom's father, whom we called Colonel Manson, was a big game guide. I think he came to Lillooet before the First World War and had enough money to buy the choice piece of property that he later left to Tom. Much of my knowledge of the local area, the folklore, and the gossip about the townspeople came from my visits and chats with Tom Manson. I trusted his judgment implicitly.

Tom said, "I remember Charlie Owens real well. He was a very interesting fellow to talk to. He had lots of stories to tell."

"Where did he come from?" I asked. "I never heard much about him except that he was Bobby Hurley's grandfather."

"Well," Tom said, "Charlie Owens told me that he came

from the USA. He said he walked all the way from Seattle"—
or was it Blaine? —"to Lillooet with a backpack full of needles,
threads, buttons, and hooks to peddle to the locals. 'I was just
bored with life,' he said, 'and I thought I would head North
into Kennedy.'" Tom grinned and said Charlie mispronounced
"Canada" as "Kennedy."

"Did he come to Lillooet?" I asked.

"Yes," said Tom, "and he stayed around for quite a while.
Got himself work on Dickey's ranch near Texas Creek. Then
he got a job cooking for the government road gangs. The men
really liked his cooking, especially his egg custards, so he
figured he'd get some experience working as a second cook in
See Hing Lung's restaurant here in Lillooet. He was good, and
became a fully-fledged cook. That's what Charlie did. I used to
like his raisin pie."

"I never remembered him being in Lillooet," I said.

"No," said Tom, "he left before you were born. He had a
plan in mind. He thought someday he'd like to get married and
start a family, but he felt he'd have to make more money first,
so he got a job as a cook in the Bralorne mining camp. He
eventually married one of the Jorgensen girls from Lillooet,
and the two made a good living cooking together in the camps.
They had one child, a daughter who married Tommy Hurley
down here in Lillooet and became your pal Bobby Hurley's
mother."

"And Charlie Owens became Bobby's grandfather," I
added.

"That is right," agreed Tom.

"I remember seeing Bobby's mother here a few times when
I called on Bobby to play or go fishing with me," I said. "But
how did Charlie Owens ever land up in Gold Bridge?'

"Well, Charlie's wife died," said Tom, "and he continued on
cooking by himself, eventually ending up as the cook in the
Gold Bridge bunkhouse."

"My brother Allan said that while he was splitting wood for

the madam and her girls, he saw Mr. Owens going in and out of the whorehouse quite a few times," I volunteered.

"Well, yes," Tom went on, a grin creasing his face. "Charlie was a regular customer, even in old age, and I asked him one time if he wasn't too old for Madam's girls. He just laughed and said he did need a bit of help now and then, but he carried a battery in his hip pocket to take care of such emergencies."

I laughed. "They didn't have Viagra back then. But how did it work—the battery?"

"I never figured out the battery method," Tom said. "And no, we didn't have Viagra, but we did have Spanish Fly!"

Our family's time in Gold Bridge was a short but colourful episode, and I look back on it very fondly. After our brief adventure in Gold Bridge, however, we moved back to the town of Lillooet in 1932. I was seven years old.

FOUR
MY BOYHOOD PAL, CLIFFORD JIM

"Hey, Gordon, you wanna go to Jim Sook's for clam chowder today?"

The question came from my companion, intrepid Hing Jim, or as he was known by his English name, Clifford Jim. It was a strange request to me at the time, because it was the first time Clifford had ever mentioned Jim Sook's clam chowder, a gustatory delight which would became a sporadic luxury item in my childhood diet in the months to come. Clifford's act of introducing me to Jim Sook's clam chowder started a ritual, though a short-term one, which is now a cherished item in my childhood memory bank.

Jim Sook, clam chowder chef extraordinaire, operated the town laundry next door to Wo Hing's general store on Lillooet's Main Street. Seven of the stores in the main block of town were owned and operated by Chinese Lillooet pioneers: two general stores, three cafés, a barbershop and a shoemaker shop. There was even a special Chinese cemetery, from whence the deceased's bones were later disinterred and sent back to China.

I knew nothing about these Chinese settlers except that they were, like the rest of us non-indigenous people, immigrants to North America and British Columbia. Many of the Chinese farm labourers were from Guangdong—Canton—province in southeastern coastal China, and the store owners may have come from Hong Kong. If and when one such member of a family made a good start in BC, he could send money to a male relative for his fare and to pay the head tax. If he wanted to be married, he had to import a wife as well, either from China, Victoria, or Vancouver. The head tax was five hundred dollars, the equivalent of one man's yearly earnings. Needless to say, this racist government policy meant that very few of these Chinese men were able to sponsor relatives. Many were forced to live out their lives in Canada as bachelors.

These men who came from Asia as immigrant labourers contributed a lot to the construction of the Canadian Pacific Railway (CPR). Many of them lost their lives in explosions and rock slides.

During the first thirteen years of my life, I grew up in close contact with two Chinese families: the Jim family and the Wing family. The Jim family, consisting of two adults and six children, was of pure Chinese extraction. The father, Jim San, was the owner-operator of Jim brothers' general store on Main Street. He was from Hong Kong, and his wife Jane was from Victoria, BC. Their children were bilingual like them, fluent in both Cantonese and English.

Our mothers, Nina Whitney and Jane Jim, were close friends and, serendipitously, pregnant at the same time in 1924. Mrs. Jim was carrying Hing in her womb, and my mother was carrying me in hers. The two pregnant mothers were in the habit of meeting in front of the Jim brothers' store before going inside to gossip over a cup of tea in Mrs. Jim's dining room. After gestation, they gave birth to two boys: me, Gordon, in December 1925, and Clifford Jim in March 1926, three months later.

Today, Clifford and I both live in the Vancouver area, and we often meet at Metrotown in South Burnaby. I greet him with, "Well, old friend, we are still 'bumping into each to each other.'"

Cliff always counters with, "Remember how, as kids, we used to pretend that we secretly talked to each other before we were born, when our mothers used to 'bump into each other' on the street? If only they had known that you and I used to communicate in code by tapping on their tummy walls."

And I jokingly add, "Yes, you could say that we were almost womb-mates in the Elementary School of Gestation." Clifford and I, in our ninety-fourth year, are the last survivors in each of our families.

Clifford's siblings each had a Chinese and an English name: Chinese for home use and English for public and especially school use: Clara, a.k.a. Ying; Victoria, a.k.a. Lin; May (in both Chinese and English); Lola, a.k.a. Lon; and Harvey, a.k.a. Yin. A good half of the second floor of Jim brothers' store contained the living quarters for the growing Jim family.

Clifford and I became lifelong friends, and with Clifford as a playmate, I developed a close connection with the Chinese community. The Caucasian community was very unsympathetic toward "Orientals," but I, due to my contact with the Jims and the Wings, became accustomed to Asian courtesy and to the respect that children showed their elders. Failure of a child to obey these two rules resulted in punishment by parents.

I was a shy child. Clifford was brash and, being a Chinese boy, was always accepted into any of the Chinese stores in Lillooet. As Clifford's fellow traveller, I was accepted too. One group of eight elderly Chinese men met every Saturday in the kitchen of See Hing Lung's restaurant to prepare a big lunch. Clifford used to take me in to see these men preparing their food, mainly freshly killed chickens and vegetables from Mrs. Foster's farm.

I recall watching an elderly man use a knife point to puncture the skin of a chicken. He inserted a straw into the hole and blew to inflate a small patch of skin. Then he carefully plucked out all the pinfeathers with his thumbnail and index fingernail.

I moved closer to him and asked him why he was going to all that trouble. "My mother never bothers to do that when she roasts a chicken."

He replied, "Chicken skin very good tasty part of chicken for us, so every time, we remove all little baby feather. They not taste good for us. Maybe when your mama roast chicken, hot oven take away bad taste, but we like boiling chicken. No good to eat baby feather—baby feather taste bad."

As five- and six-year-olds, we spent Sundays exploring the back porches of a few businesses that fronted on Main Street. I was unafraid of reprimand, being as I was with bold Clifford, and we climbed over fences to gain access to backyards, looking for scraps of wood or cardboard to take to the dugout cabin we had built with the twins, Peter and Paul Larter, on the hillside behind Lillooet. We were probably known to all the proprietors of the stores as two stupid little kids who liked to rummage through garbage on back porches.

I remember, too, finding discarded, unsaleable oranges and grapefruit sporting a spot of greenish mould. I simply cut away these spots with my pocket knife. I was told that oranges and grapefruit were high in vitamin C. And I remember finding black bananas, which no one in his right mind would spend a nickel on because they weren't yellow, but the fruit inside was great— well, a bit overripe, but as sweet as honey.

Of course Clifford thought I was nutty, but I wasn't. I was simply hungry. To a boy on welfare, oranges and bananas and grapefruit were luxury items. And hey, maybe my boyhood diet of penicillin-infected fruit and overripe bananas is one of the reasons I am still in good health today at ninety-four. (A friend of mine, Courtenay Grey, used to pick up black bananas from the rear of his local Safeway store in Burnaby and turn them it into homemade banana wine. He could have marketed it as "Grey's Banan-o Noir.")

Many stores in Lillooet had small backyards without porches, but the Park brothers' store, because of its rapid turnover of perishables, required a large porch for stacking unsaleable vegetables and fruit, which we city dwellers nowadays call useless garbage.

But this useless garbage was taken away late each Sunday afternoon by an elderly Chinese farm worker known to Cliff and me as Chang. He was one of five Chinese farm labourers who worked on Mrs. Foster's farm, located right below the town on a large cultivated glacial bench bordering the Fraser River.

Chang and his four Chinese co-workers lived rent-free in a small shack in a corner of Mrs. Foster's farm. Here, they were allowed to grow vegetables and raise a few pigs.

It was Chang's chore to visit the back porches of the Parks' store on Sunday to pick up two forty-gallon used oil cans with a wooden yoke apparatus—its arms wonderfully padded to fit snugly around the back of his neck—and carry home the spoiled produce.

We watched him perform this feat several times. With the apparatus, he would pick up the two buckets, balancing them, testing their weight, and trotting away, carrying the load down to his shack on Mrs. Foster's farm. Chang and his co-workers used the garbage or slop to fatten up the half a dozen pigs they reared every year.

Clifford and I were fascinated by Chang's method of dancing and trotting downhill, the two buckets of garbage bouncing in time with his spritely trot. And I was very impressed with Chang, a slight, skinny old man carrying two heavily loaded buckets to the Foster farm a good half mile away.

Every Monday morning, Chang returned the empty,

spotlessly cleaned buckets to the back porch of the Parks' store, ready for a refill of slop.

One of our favourite visiting stops was Jim Sook's laundry. It was located at the west end of the string of stores and shops on Main Street.

Mr. Jim Sook had developed a lucrative business doing the weekly laundry for three cafés, one hotel, and eight auto courts, all on Main Street. He also serviced a select group of rich Lillooet residents, who disdained to be seen hanging out their washing on a clothesline. There were no electric clothes dryers in Lillooet at that time.

Clifford and I used to ask Jim Sook if we could watch him iron freshly washed shirts, sheets, pillowcases, tablecloths, fancy napkins for the hotel, curtains, or barbershop aprons. He was always kind enough to seat us on chairs so we could watch.

I was always greatly amused when it came time for Jim Sook to iron the starched collars and cuffs of men's dress shirts. He would make a mixture of cornstarch and warm water in a jug, and when the contents were mixed to his satisfaction, he'd take in a huge mouthful of the starchy fluid, both cheeks bulging, and then, bending over his ironing board, blow a fine spray with great force out through his pursed lips and onto the cuffs and collars of the shirts he was going to iron. After the spray dried sufficiently, he expertly ironed each article.

I thought it was a good thing that his customers never witnessed his wonderful oral spray technique.

I admired, too, his electric iron. My mother had to heat a heavy, detachable iron on the stovetop before reattaching its wooden handle. Iron, reheat with handle detached, reattach handle, continue ironing… It was tedious work compared to Jim Sook's electric operation.

Jim Sook was a handsome bachelor who obviously liked children. I knew he liked Clifford and me. When he paused at noon to cook his lunch, he would sometimes ask us if we would like to eat a bowl of clam chowder with him. He made a delicious clam chowder. I remember that he opened two tin cans containing large clams. Today, one can buy only tiny baby canned clams.

We two very persistent bums often invited ourselves back for clam chowder at "Jim Sook's free restaurant." He never refused us his hospitality. Clifford and I graciously thanked him after each meal: "Thank you very much, Mr. Sook. You make the best clam chowder in the whole wide world."

We reached school age, a year passed, and we somehow no longer visited Jim Sook. I must confess that I missed his friendship and I missed his clam chowder. So, one Saturday morning on our usual prowl, I suggested to Clifford that we visit Jim Sook again to watch him work. I hoped he would, as in the past, offer us a bowl of his delicious clam chowder.

Clifford agreed. So at eleven thirty, we went around to the back door of his shop and knocked.

This time, instead of Jim Sook coming to the door, there appeared a tall, pretty, haughty-looking young Chinese woman, glaring down at us with piercing, angry eyes.

I was at a loss for words. Clifford covered his mouth with his hand and whispered to me, "Jeezus, I forgot to tell you that Jim Sook got married one month ago."

Jim Sook's wife took a step toward us, peered down, and asked in a loud, shrill voice, "What. You. Want?"

I was speechless, abashed to say the least, but Clifford said matter-of-factly, "Can we come in for a bowl of clam chowder, please, Mrs. Sook?"

She screamed, *"Jooo hoyyy laaa!"* and slammed the door in our faces.

I ran. Cliff caught up with me on the street, laughing his head off.

"What did she say? I stammered.

"She said in Chinese, 'Go away, you little beggars!'"

It sounded more like she meant to say, "Go away, you little buggers!"

That ended our friendly relations with gentle, kind Jim Sook. I never asked Clifford whether or not Jim Sook had children of his own. Maybe he did, and maybe he cooked clam chowder for them.

FIVE

GAMES AND TOYS OF THE DEPRESSION ERA

Today's children are inundated with a plethora of electronic games, toys, and smart phones, activities that can be enjoyed by oneself. As a Depression child, my playmates and I were lucky, in a way, because we learned from older children and siblings how to create toys out of almost nothing. If one of us children showed up with a new creation, the others would make copies, and we would continue to play together. We weren't bent over our smart phones, texting each other across the twenty feet that separated us.

One activity we shared was called tin can horseshoes. Not to be confused with the traditional throwing game of horseshoes, our horseshoes game was an immediate success because it involved creating, out of junk and at no cost, a very noisy toy. We kids loved to make noise. Usually girls didn't opt to play this game. It was too noisy, too unladylike.

As a Lillooet five-year-old in 1930, I went to the tin can garbage dump on the outskirts of the town unless I had what I needed in my own garbage can. I would select two empty Pacific milk cans with both metal ends intact. It wouldn't work if one end had been removed by a can opener. I always made sure they were clean inside, and if they weren't, I gave them a quick rinse under the water faucet. When milk is left in the bottom of an empty can, it can go sour and really start to stink!

I would take the two cans out onto a concrete or wooden sidewalk, a section of driveway, or a roadway safe from traffic. Then I would place one can beside each foot at a right angle to my shoe, which pointed forward.

Tin Can Horseshoes

Now came the magic part, the fun part. I lifted my left foot so that it was resting gently on the can beside it, then, with all my strength, I would stomp on the can with my left shoe. Lo and behold, the ends of the dented can would curl up and grab onto each side of my shoe. After a few more stomps, the can was now stuck, and if I lifted my shoe, the can would come with it.

I repeated the same procedure with my right foot. Sometimes I had to hang on to something solid—maybe a friend or a fence post—while I stood on my left foot in its new milk can horseshoe. After stomping on the right-hand can, I now had two tin can horseshoes, one on each foot.

With my arms outstretched, or holding a stick in one hand for support, I was free to stomp down the hard road, pleased at the loud noises coming from my brand-new tin can horseshoes. I didn't stomp on a soft surface like dirt because I wouldn't make any noise.

People would sit up and notice! My friends and I were proud of ourselves, even if people did complain about the noise we were creating. The noise was, after all, the whole reason for making this wonderful toy.

There was another game my friends and I played that was more sedate than tin can horseshoes and easier to make equipment for, though not suited for toddlers. We called it Tippicat. Whence came that title, I have no idea.

The equipment consisted of two parts: the tippicat, and the handle or swatter. First I would find an unused softwood broom handle in good condition. I would not steal it from my mother's broom closet.

With a small handsaw, I would saw off a three-inch piece from one end of the broom handle and mark off three one-inch sections with a pencil. On each end, one third of the length of the three-inch cylinder, I used a sharp knife to whittle two one-inch, cone-shaped ends. Gently, with a wood rasp and sandpaper, I'd smooth off each of the two whittled end cones. And that was the tippicat. I would use the remainder of the broom handle as the bat or swatter.

Now I was ready to play. Any number of male or female contestants could play. To play, we took turns placing our three-inch tippicat on the start line someone had drawn in the soil or on the lawn. On my turn, I took my swatter and addressed the tippicat on the ground in front of me. Grasping the swatter in both hands as I would a baseball bat, but remembering that I would make a downward, chopping stroke instead of a horizontal swing, I took aim at the front end of the conical tippicat and swung. If my aim was true, my tippicat would spin up into the air in front of me, and I would strike the whole body of the tippicat with my swatter, sending it flying up and forward, as far down the playing field as possible. Then I would run ahead and stick one conical end of my tippicat into the soil—ready, as a marker, for my next swat. Each player was allowed the same number of swings, and the one whose tippicat travelled the greatest total distance from the start line won the match. To me it didn't matter who won. My great pleasure came from knowing I could make such a beautiful, wonderful toy with my own hands.

Many children's toys—a model aeroplane, for example—would be too complicated to describe without an accompanying diagram. But making a slingshot was simpler and needs no diagram.

The wood had to be carefully chosen. Lillooet was quite small, population seven hundred. The main forests behind Lillooet included lodgepole and ponderosa pines and some fir trees. Domestic orchards included numerous fruit trees introduced by residents, such as apple, cherry, peach, nectarine, prune, plum, and apricot. (The common way to eat an apricot fresh off the branch involved spitting out the pit onto the ground. So today, Lillooet teems with apricot trees planted orally by humans in backyards and empty lots.)

But there were also, on the side hills, wild deciduous trees such as the saskatoon tree, local Indian name *tsaqwem*, which provided delicious berry fruit and excellent material for homemade fishing poles and other carved objects like pea whistles. It was my favourite source of wood for a catapult or slingshot with its Y-shaped "crutch" (crotch) construction. I remember scanning such trees for a suitable Y-shaped branch section, and when I had found one, I waited until it had grown to the right size and then cut it off with my jackknife.

This liberated crutch section consisted of a half-inch thick, Y-shaped section of a saskatoon branch. The bottom portion of the section, the stem of the Y, was preferably an inch thick to provide a sturdy enough piece to fit into my left hand. And the two upper forks of the Y section had to be thick enough, strong enough, for the attachment of the power source of the slingshot: two rubber bands, one band on each arm. Finally, I would attach a leather pouch, a receptacle for round stone projectiles, to the ends of the two dangling rubber bands.

I usually liberated the rubber bands by cutting off strips from a worn-out car's inner tube using a pair of sturdy shears. The leather pouch came from the tongue of an abandoned, worn-out leather shoe. When the three parts — the wooden Y, the two dangling rubber bands, and the leather pouch — were assembled, the whole weapon could be snugly fitted into a rear pocket of my blue jeans and or into one of my jacket pockets. My other jacket pocket could be stuffed full of round stones, my ammunition. I was ready for target practice on a row of tin cans on a fence rail.

Can you picture David facing Goliath with his primitive sling, winding up and hitting the giant Philistine between the eyes with a lethal sling stone? In the time it took David to launch his one stone, I, with my modern rubber-powered slingshot, could have hit Goliath three or four times.

Using a slingshot was fast and easy: I held the crutch in my left hand, placed a stone into the pouch with my right, and squeezed my hold on the stone as I raised my left hand to aim the slingshot while pulling back hard on the rubber bands as far as my right ear. Then I would release the pouch, and the potential energy stored in the stretched rubber bands flung my first shot at the chosen target.

Making a kite was also easy, if one had a few simple raw materials: two cedar sticks; stretchy crepe paper left over from Christmas decorations; some store string for making a frame for the paper to be pasted onto; some homemade water-and-flour paste; and a couple hundred feet of stout salmon-fishing twine for launching and tethering. When I was nine years old, and our family moved to the Cayoosh flats, there was a constant breeze blowing from west to east. So once my kite was in the air — a really beautiful sight — it stayed up in the air until the twine broke, or it rained, or the breeze temporarily slackened. Worse, if somebody stole it in the night, or during the day when I was in school, it would be gone forever. When that happened, and it happened often, I was pissed off, sore as hell for a while. But then I was as proud as a peacock of my recognized skill as a kite-maker. Nobody ever stole a poorly made, un-flyable kite. Mine were always first-class kite masterpieces.

I also made my own helicopters, modelled on the winged seeds of maple trees. I was taught how to use tin snips — scissors for cutting metal — and cut tin from cans and pails into helicopter blades. I also learned how to use part of a broom handle for a hand grip, how to use a beheaded spike for an axle, and how to mount the propeller on the spool using tiny finishing nails, an empty thread spool as a rotor, and cotton twine. What pride and what joy came from creating such a magnificent toy. And what absorbing fun, watching it rise from your hands into the air and glide gently back to the ground.

We loved making peapod boats. When it rained and created mud puddles, we children used to extract the pea seeds from a green peapod without damaging the boat-like peapod itself. Then, using tiny broken parts of a toothpick or a matchstick for thwarts, we built miniature fleets of peapod boats, ready to be gently pushed through the water by a stick or blown back and forth by the breath from our pursed lips.

We also made our own type of Frisbee by "sailing" the lids

of lard pails, jam tins, and Roger's golden syrup cans. I would stand out in the school playground, hold out a lid between my thumb and index finger, and, with a backhand motion, fling it into the air. Then I'd watch it come back to earth, waiting to be picked up again and sailed into the wild blue yonder. We never tried to catch these Frisbees in the air, however, because their metal edges could inflict pain, or even cut and draw blood.

We could play many games in our town that could never be played in a city because of car traffic. Lillooet was blessed with a paucity of cars and car traffic—a new Ford sedan cost as much as eight hundred dollars!—so children could play in the street until a slow-moving car came into view. We could play marbles or Prisoner's Base, a kind of tag that involved running back and forth from the sidewalk out into the street. Common, too, was piggyback jousting. Two small boys, the jousters, mounted on the backs of two large boys, the steeds, and provided bystanders with exciting, almost medieval entertainment. You lost if you were knocked or pulled off your horse by your antagonist. Then someone would shout, "Car coming, car coming," and we would all scurry back onto the sidewalk.

Model aeroplane building was a definite passion with preteen boys in Lillooet. My older brother Ernie, eight years my senior, was mechanically gifted. Albert Larter, the blacksmith's son, had taught him how to solder metal pieces together using lead solder, a soldering iron, and a pump-up gasoline blowtorch. Since the red-hot solder had to be heated by a blowtorch flame, Albert coached Ernie on technique and design but didn't allow him to prepare and light the blowtorch.

Nevertheless, Ernie produced a light sheet-metal model aeroplane that looked so real it even had wheels to land on. He let me look at it, but never let me touch it. It was too precious, and was never left out of his sight while I was around. I wanted to hold it and "pretend fly" it around the room. One afternoon, I was out in our backyard, watching my mother rake up some grass clippings, when a seaplane two thousand feet up in the air came into view. It was preparing to descend and land on Seton Lake, three and a half miles to the west of town. I tugged at my mother's skirt and pointed up at the aeroplane, pleading, "Hurry, hurry, Mommy, before it gets away! Reach up with your rake and hook it down for me!"

Those were happy days!

Fourteen-year-old Gordon with his model
airplane.

SIX

THE CAYOOSH FLATS AND THE TULIPS

My maternal grandparents, Effie and Harry Reynolds, came to
Lillooet in 1918 and squatted on a small piece of land on the
Cayoosh flats, one hundred feet below the town flat of Lillooet.
The town flat, like so many other flats along the Fraser River,
was located on an old lake bed left behind by the last ice age
ten thousand years ago. The snow on the mountains behind
Lillooet provides, to this day, meltwater that flows on the
surface as creeks or underground as aquifers.

Smaller creeks emptying into the Fraser, such as Cayoosh
Creek, had incised their glacial deposits in their own narrow
valleys, leaving behind some small strips of arable land on their
banks. Harry and Effie, immigrants from the USA, squatted
on such a piece of land where Cayoosh Creek empties into the
Fraser. Unfortunately, whenever the Fraser River flooded in
springtime, as it often did, it caused Cayoosh Creek to back up
and erode a small amount of the arable land my grandparents
and two neighbours had squatted on.

My grandparents and their neighbours were fortunate,
however, because an aquifer exited from the very bottom of the
town flat cliff and provided them with enough water for
drinking and watering their vegetable gardens. At other times,

51

such as Monday wash days, they had to carry water in buckets from the creek, a distance of about one hundred yards (one hundred metres).

Cayoosh Creek also supplied my energetic grandparents with a constant supply of firewood in the form of driftwood, which had accumulated over the years in small bays along the creek or floated twenty-five miles downstream from Duffy Lake, the headwaters of Cayoosh Creek.

My grandparents' two neighbours were too lazy to expend the necessary effort involved in harvesting driftwood. They were content to buy firewood from Otto Hendrickson, town woodcutter and purveyor of precut blocks ready to be split into firewood.

Our grandfather, with the help of my older brother Ernie, who was living with the grandparents full time, had to rescue floating driftwood logs from the creek or pull them out from behind rocks, then pile them on the banks to dry out before sawing them into useable lengths. Then they either dragged or wheeled those smaller lengths the hundred yards or so to the fence of my grandparents' property. The wood lay in the open air and dried in large piles until it was needed for firewood, or until my brother was in the mood to split logs.

They sawed the logs into stove-length blocks about eighteen inches long and then split them into quarters with a sledgehammer and a steel wedge. Often they left the blocks outside their property, along with a large number of freshly split quarters and an equal amount of firewood sticks. My brother, however, because he was the axeman, noticed that from time to time, firewood was disappearing from where he had carefully stacked it.

So when he had free time after school, he completed the time-consuming process of moving quarters from outside the fence to inside their yard, where they could be more readily split into firewood. He wheeled load after load of blocks in through the front gate and around to the side yard, dumping them beside their very large chopping block, formerly the butt end of a huge log that had floated down from Duffy Lake. Remember that the portable chainsaw had not yet been invented, so everything to do with firewood had to done by hand. It was labour intensive in the extreme.

I was fascinated, watching my older brother split the blocks into quarters and then firewood using sledge and wedge. I was so very anxious to learn that manly skill. So, at the age of eight, I was taught by my older brother to carefully place a quarter of a block "upright" onto the big chopping block, where it could be split with difficulty and great skill into smaller sticks for the kitchen stove.

The usual—and safe—procedure for doing this was to stand the quarter block on the chopping block, back away, and then, gripping the long axe handle comfortably with both hands, bring the axe down on the top surface of the block to split off smaller pieces that would fit into the firebox of the stove. My older brother taught me the whole process of converting blocks into quarters, and quarters into firewood. It was a slow process because after each split, the quarter-block had to be stood up again for another skillful blow from the axe.

Soon, under the cautious eye of my older brother, I was shown a shortcut technique. "Hold the quarter block steady with your *left hand*, being careful to keep your fingers out of the way. Then, using only your *right hand* and a shortened grip on the axe handle, bring the axe down and chop the quarter block into pieces of firewood."

It looked dangerous, and it was dangerous. Some people lost fingers that way. Grandfather had been lucky. He had only split his left thumb lengthwise, almost in two. After a few weeks, the two halves grew back together. It was an ugly thumb to look at, like two thumbs glued together.

I personally confess that I achieved mastery of the shortcut technique and remember it with great pleasure. I was a whiz at cutting firewood. (Stop looking at my left hand!)

You will have come by now to understand what a precious commodity firewood was. Townfolk had to buy their firewood by the cord, in pre-sawn blocks or short logs, from whoever was illegally cutting down ponderosa pine trees on the East River flat across the river.

Some few homes were equipped with electricity, which was suitable for cooking, baking, and heating water. But even those families had to buy illegal wood for their fireplaces or circulating wood stoves.

One day, my brother looked at the neat stack of firewood with suspicion. It had shrunk considerably. Almost six armloads of firewood were gone from the carefully marked stack. How could that be? He concluded that someone was stealing his grandparents' firewood. Could it be the Doneghys who lived next door upstream? Or Roy Doherty, who lived next door downstream? No way!

Then he remembered that Roy Doherty had moved away recently, and new neighbours had moved in, the Tulip family. Could they be the ones robbing his woodpile? He counted the number of sticks in the stack once more. He would check again in the morning.

Next morning, before he left for school, he checked and found everything in order. The woodpile remained intact that week.

On Friday night after supper, the Tulips came to call and get acquainted, and were invited in for tea. Mrs. Tulip explained her lifelong passion for rug making. She had an adjustable wooden frame her husband had made for her, on which she could stretch the desired size of burlap for whichever type of rug she was making. She explained how she dyed her white wool into various colours and how similar her technique was to crocheting.

My grandmother was good at crocheting and adept at knitting. Most of our winter clothing — socks, sweaters, mitts, parkas, and toques — were knitted by womenfolk whose families couldn't afford ready-made clothing from the local stores or mail order from the T. Eaton Company.

"Yes," Mrs. Tulip said, when she was questioned by my grandfather. "We are friends of Ma Murray, a wonderful, wonderful woman." I knew that Ma Murray was the owner of the local newspaper, the *Bridge River Lillooet News*, and she was the wife of the politician who represented our riding in the Victoria legislature. I also knew that she and her husband looked down on us poor folk.

The Tulips thanked their hosts for a pleasant evening and left, walking home in the dark.

Next morning, before he left for Dolly Varden fishing, my brother checked his woodpile. Holy Mackinaw! Two good armloads of firewood were missing! Now it was clear to my brother that the Tulips were stealing their firewood. So he decided to stay up at night, equipped with a powerful flashlight, and sit with the kitchen door open. This way he could see the outline of the woodpile, but more importantly, he could hear footsteps on the gravel.

For two nights he kept watch. No footsteps. No shadowy figures near the woodpile. Then, on the third night, he heard them: muffled footsteps approaching from downstream, from the Tulips' property. They were nearing the woodpile.

Then... silence!

He stealthily climbed over the fence, avoiding the noisy gate with its rusty hinges, and moved as rapidly and silently as possible along the path between the woodpile and the Tulips' property. He needn't have been so very quiet because the Tulips, their arms laden with firewood, were noisily huffing and puffing their nefarious way homeward.

My brother soon caught up, ran around them, and, stopping three feet in front, shone his powerful flashlight in their faces.

The Tulips were stunned! They paused. They dropped their stolen firewood. They bolted. They ran homeward.

My brother ran after them, yelling and waving his flashlight at their backs.

He chased them to their front gate, and as they stumbled toward their back door, he shouted after them, "You'd better bring back all the firewood you stole from my grandparents, or else!"

He must have had something planned in the back of his mind because he certainly knew they could not bring back even one stick of stolen firewood. They had already burned it.

He waited a few seconds, then turned and headed back to our grandparents' front gate, where he stopped and looked back to where the Tulips had dropped their stolen firewood. He spoke aloud to himself. "Leave it there. Let it remind them of their theft, the goddamn rotten thieves. They won't dare go near it, and anyone passing by will wonder how it got there."

A week passed, and the Tulips were unseen on the Cayoosh flats. They may have been severely frightened by my brother's last words: *or else*. So frightened that they chose to remain indoors.

Around noon, my grandfather said, "Maybe they are packing, getting ready to move away."

"I hope they do," said Grandmother.

Without saying a word to anyone, my brother, at dusk that day, took down his twenty-two-calibre rifle from the wall in his bedroom and put two cartridges in the watch pocket of his blue jeans. With the rifle tucked under his left arm, he quietly left the house and crept low along the back fence to the corner joining the Tulips' property to our grandparents'. Once there, he rested his rifle on top of the corner fence post, checking to see if he could get a clear view of the Tulips' kitchen stovepipe against the dimly lit sky. Yes, he could see the stovepipe as clear as a bell!

My brother was a crack shot. He deftly loaded his rifle, rested it on the top of the fence post, and shot his first bullet through a spot six inches from the top of the stovepipe.

Quickly he ejected the spent shell casing, calmly reloaded, and placed a second bullet twelve inches below the first. The sound of the two bullets hitting the stove pipe must have been deafening to the occupants of the house.

Where would a third shot strike?

Two days later at nine o'clock in the morning, a moving van pulled up in front of the Tulips' front gate. Two men quickly loaded the van and, with the Tulips sitting on chairs in the back, drove away.

My brother grinned at our grandfather. "I don't know what prompted them to leave, but I don't think they'll be back!"

Ernie and Allan sawing firewood at grandfather's place

SEVEN
GRANDMOTHER

My maternal grandmother, Effie Reynolds, was born in 1873 in Culdesac, a small town in Idaho. Idaho touches the Canadian border at eastern British Columbia, along the forty-ninth parallel of latitude.

Effie met my grandfather during the exciting days of the Klondike Gold Rush. By then, she was in her mid-twenties and had moved to Dawson City, which was teaming with Americans at the time. When she and Harry Reynolds met, they decided to return to Idaho and became farmers. Effie was a very enterprising woman. She was born and raised on a farm, and as she grew up, she became familiar with the many aspects of agriculture connected to the kitchen. She was taught to be a good cook, as were most girls of her generation. And as a cook, she and her mother and sisters were responsible for the kitchen garden. She was helped by the menfolk in the preparation and tilling of the soil, but after she had planted the seeds for all of her chosen vegetables, such as carrots, string beans, peas, potatoes, cooking onions and green onions, lettuce, tomatoes, beets, parsnips, radishes, cucumbers, squash, and cabbage, she was responsible for weed control, watering, insect control, and, of course, harvesting the berries.

When they arrived in Lillooet, she and my grandfather settled on the banks of the Cayoosh Creek, and she carried with her all the traditions she had learned as a girl.

Effie was very interested in cultivating berries, such as currants—white, red, and black varieties—raspberries, both red and pink, and a strange type of berry she called deadly nightshade, which wasn't poisonous in the least but had a very, very strong flavour. I was very fond of it.

I remember that nightshade berries, when preserved in Mason jars with added sugar, tasted like the dark blue ink we students used in the elementary classroom. A chemist would be able to name the pertinent chemicals in both the berry and the ink. The ink had to be non-poisonous, of course, because we children invariably went home from school with ink-stained hands. I remember always getting ink on my right hand from the pen nib after I had dipped it into the inkwell located in the top right-hand corner of each desk. Invariably, my blue-stained fingers would come into contact with my mouth, and I became accustomed to the taste. If the ink had been mixed with sugar, I swear it could have passed for deadly nightshade juice.

In the growing season, my grandparents were in the garden at dawn, adjusting the water, making sure each row got its share. They had a special way of weeding. Rather than bending or kneeling to pluck out weeds or cutting them with a hoe, they each straddled a stool, weeding from the top of a row to the bottom, plucking and cutting young weeds with the sharpened hoe blade.

Important to her garden was the chicken manure she garnered from her chicken coop, which sheltered her six hundred laying hens of the Plymouth Rock and Rhode Island Red varieties. Each morning, after the hens were ushered into the wheat-scattered yard, the floor of the chicken poop was cleaned from the coop with a hoe, shovelled into a big bucket, carried to the garden fence, and dumped to make a new pile that sat and ripened over the winter. I remember her putting my childish hands on top of the manure pile in the winter, so I could feel the heat from the bacterial action within. It was really hot if you thrust your hand a few inches into the pile. And smelly, too! Every year in autumn, Grandfather dug a hole in the new manure pile and filled it with loam. Then Grandmother inserted rhubarb roots from a mother plant in the garden. The heat from the composting chicken manure guaranteed an early rhubarb crop every spring. Near the end of spring and the beginning of summer, her visitors enjoyed her rhubarb-apple pie, one of my favourite pies even today.

My grandmother was an excellent cook. Her steel-hinged baking storage box next to the big wood-burning stove was always filled with loaves of bread, cinnamon buns, and coffee cake.

Her six hundred hens produced enough eggs that my teenage aunt Ruby could deliver the excess by hand, in a lidded bucket, twice a week to Jim brothers' uptown. In the Hungry Thirties a dozen eggs retailed for thirty cents a dozen, a paltry sum today. I think Grandmother received fifteen cents per dozen. Of course bread, in those days, cost a dime a loaf. A shave and a haircut cost seventy-five cents. (Notice that in typing, I avoid using dollar signs. We couldn't afford dollar signs in the Depression.)

I remember the dozens of baby chicks that appeared each spring, hatched from the eggs which had been fertilized — the rooster's daily task — and placed in the heated incubator. My grandparents didn't have electricity, and I can't remember how they heated the incubator. Maybe they used an oil lamp for heat. Maybe they placed the incubator in a corner of the large kitchen.

Sometimes a renegade hen would appear from the bushland bordering the chicken yard, a dozen baby chicks peep-peeping behind her. There was always a danger of the chicks being spied by the ubiquitous chicken hawks patrolling overhead. But a big hawk was more interested in taking away the mother hen, a decent-sized meal. Sometimes my older brother would shoot down unwary hawks. But a new hawk always seemed to replace the deceased bird in a week or so. However, the loss of a mother was not a problem. The motherless chicks were simply added to the incubator flock of new chicks in the henhouse.

My grandmother kept a close watch on each hen's egg-laying efficiency. Poor producers ended up on our dinner plates as chicken stew. I remember my grandmother showing me the tiny eggs in the ovary of a poor layer. She put them in the stew to show me. I ate them with satisfaction, bolstered by my new knowledge of the need for seashells in a hen's diet. The hen's ovary, Grandmother explained, was like an assembly line. The miniature eggs grew in size, adding white albumen to the yellow yolk, the whole to be encased in a calcareous egg shell. It was necessary to feed crushed seashells to the hens for their ovaries to produce shelled eggs.

Years later, when my wife Joanne and I were visiting a family in Croatia, the grandmother there — Baka, she was called — was showing me her small chicken coop in their backyard. It contained her five newly purchased hens. Baka complained that the hens weren't laying any eggs. So I asked her, in my limited, freshly learned Croatian, to show me their feed. I saw immediately that there was no seashell mixed with the wheat, so I made quick survey of her vegetable garden and found three large snails. I brought them to Baka and explained that the hens needed a chemical, calcium carbonate, to create eggshells in their ovaries. Snail shells and chicken eggshells, I explained, were made of the same chemical material. After I cracked the shells by stepping on them, I scraped up their mess with a stick and tossed them to the hens, who gobbled them up in a few seconds. Baka and I then went around her backyard and found a dozen more large snails. We took them back to the henhouse, where I cracked the shells with a stone and fed all the crushed remains to the hens. The hens ravenously ate the crushed snail shell and flesh.

Next morning at the breakfast table, Baka proudly showed us five fresh eggs, one egg from each hen, which she cooked and proudly portioned out to us. She told her family excitedly in Croatian how she and I had found the snails, cracked them open, and fed them to the chickens. I added that we had used up all the available snails in the backyard, but Milan, her son-in-law, could buy a large sack of crushed clamshells in the local supermarket for a few dinars per pound. Clamshell is similar to snail shell—that's Biology 101. Milan did so that very day, and Baka's problem with egg production was solved. Thus my grandmother's knowledge in 1933 was passed to Baka the Croatian grandmother fifty years later, in 1983. Which came first—the chicken, or the egg, or grandmothers?

When I was four, I was left in my grandmother's care on the Cayoosh Creek flats for several weekends in the summer. I have never forgotten what happened at four o'clock one Sunday morning. Grandfather was out of town that weekend, teaching an orchard owner how to spray his apple trees to prevent a coddling moth invasion, so I was put to sleep in Grandfather and Grandmother's large bed at about eight thirty that evening. Grandmother joined me in the bed an hour or so later. I was awakened before sunrise the next morning by Grandmother suddenly heaving herself erect, climbing out of the bed, and going to the open window that faced onto the chicken coop. I heard her muffle a curse as she reached down and picked up a double-barrelled shotgun she had loaded and left leaning against the wall next to the window. I saw her pull back both hammers and poke the gun through the open window. Then: *Bwam! Bwam!* The two explosions made the room shake.

I was jolted upright. Grandmother screamed, "That will teach you *sons o' bitches* to try to steal my chickens!"

Back home on Monday, I asked my mother, "Why was Grammy swearing at somebody? Was there really someone out there in the dark, trying to steal her chickens?"

My mother replied, "Yes, there were men out there, bad men, men who work for the railroad and live in a bunkhouse up on the town flat. Bad men who sneak down after dark into Grammy's henhouse and steal chickens off their roosts. The bad men choke the chickens to death so they can't make any noise. Then they sneak back up the hill to their bunkhouse and cook Grammy's chickens the next day for their supper." I knew then that these particular PGE railway workmen never again would risk their lives for a free chicken dinner. Grandmother's shotgun psychology had taught them a life-saving lesson!

I would like to leave you with glimpse of a lighter side of my grandmother's personality by describing her behaviour at the local Sunday afternoon baseball games played on the field in front of the Lillooet secondary school. Spectators at the baseball game sat on three tiers of benches parallel to the third-base line.

Grandmother always came early to secure a seat on the ground floor—that is, on the first tier of benches. She weighed over two hundred pounds. Although she was a tall woman, she could never have hoisted her bulk up onto the second or third tier.

Her weight was matched by her tremendous enthusiasm for the game. She didn't just sit and watch the play. She often stood up from her seat in the first tier during an exciting play, waving her arms and screaming, and other spectators would suddenly find their view obstructed by Grandmother's ample height and width. Her raucous screaming blasted their ears. It was very annoying. Those around her vehemently voiced their objection to her behaviour by telling her to "sit down and shut up."

But Grandmother possessed a grand sense of humour. Being from the USA, she turned her massive presence to face her Canadian tormenters and shouted, "You Canadians are hypocrites. I go to your church Sunday morning, and the minister sings, "Stand up for Jesus!" But when I get to the ball game after lunch, you all shout, "Sit down, sit down, for Christ's sake! Make up your minds!"

EIGHT
THE WATER PISTOL FIGHT

"Okay," said Peter to his twin brother, Paul. "Now all we need is some ammunition, some water."

I was paired with Paul, and Peter was paired with John Wing. The twins could never play together as a team because they fought like a cat and dog. That was real irony, to my way of thinking, because they were named after Saint Peter and Saint Paul, Bible friends and the founders of the Christian Church in which we four were Sunday school classmates.

The four of us were combatants, getting ready for a water pistol fight on Lillooet's deserted main street one hot Monday morning in July, 1931. School was out for two months, and it was playtime for us.

Water pistol fighting, one of our favourite summer activities, was so much fun because it was so ridiculous. We had weapons, metal replicas of real Dick Tracy pistols, but they squirted water instead of bullets. After a water pistol fight, you were a mess, your face and clothing soaked with clean, fresh water. But a little water never harmed anyone permanently, did it? On a hot summer morning, we didn't mind being hit in the face or anywhere else, as long as the water didn't get into an eye, mouth, or nose. But even that was tolerable, evoking yelps of delight from the perpetrator. Squirting an opponent in the face was the very best fun, a heroic credit to one's boyhood marksmanship.

Yeah, we're ready," said Paul. "But I think Gordon's low on ammunition?"

"Well, John 'n' me have plenty of ammo," said Peter. "Milk cans full from our tap at home."

"I've got enough for a start," I said. "And I can always refuel later, somehow. Don't worry about me."

Actually, I had a secret plan, one that involved Alec Fook's shoe repair shop on Lillooet's Main Street. Alec Fook, a long-time Chinese resident of Lillooet, was the town shoemaker, one of my older male acquaintances, and one of my mentors.

I remember the first time I saw Alec. I was standing with Hing Jim, my Chinese pal, in the doorway of Alec Fook's shoe repair shop, gawking at his short, rotund figure seated in a high-backed bamboo chair. He was bending over a worn leather lace-up shoe that he had placed bottom-up on his shoemaker's iron last. He had just finished carefully ripping off, with a special tool, the shoe's worn bottom half-sole, exposing the healthy leather under it. And he was replacing the worn shoe sole with a freshly carved, soaking wet leather mate.

Then came the amazing part. His mouth bulged with small, sharp-tipped shoemaker nails, which he rapidly spat, one at a time, through his full red lips and into the thumb and forefinger of his left hand. These he placed swiftly into the new leather half-sole and deftly hammered into place with lightning strokes of his flathead shoemaker's hammer. The nails made a neat pattern around the edge of the new half-sole, fastening its new strong wetness onto the dry, receptive leather mate waiting beneath.

After I got to know him, I visited his shop from time to time. I was always fascinated, watching his hand move to and from his mouth with lightning speed, extracting shiny nails between his thumb and index finger, and—*bang bang bang*—

nailing the freshly carved new leather onto the old. Voila! An old, tired shoe was given a new sole and a new life!

How commonplace can a miracle be? Alec, and old man, brought to life his ultra-sharp leather-cutting knife by carving, again and again, perfectly-shaped, beautiful new leather cowhide half-soles out of an earthy, smelly slab of leather that had lain soaking, getting soft and carve-able, in a filthy tub of brown-stained, foul-smelling water that had never been emptied since day one.

That Friday morning, when I was almost out of ammunition for my water pistol, I crouched near the open door of Alec Fook's shoemaker shop. When I was certain that I was unseen by my fellow combatants on the street, I crept through the open doorway. With a warning hiss to my startled shoemaker friend, I pointed to my pistol, then to the tub of filthy water.

Alec Fook quickly regained his composure, grinned, and nodded. So I quickly filled my pistol and ammo can with "fermented urine" and crept furtively back outside to rejoin the water pistol war.

Needless to say, my side won the day. The opposing team surrendered in anger and disgust. "You're a rotten bastard, Gord!" Peter yelled. "Yeah, you really are a rotten bastard!" echoed John Wing.

Who was it who first said, "All's fair in love and war?" I knew I was as guilty as hell, but I was as happy as sin.

NINE
PROUD AND PREJUDICED IN LILLOOET

There was another story about Alec Fook the shoemaker that, while humorous at the time, still angers me because of what it says about Lillooet society's attitude toward the town's Chinese settlers. The summer after our water pistol fight, on a sunny Saturday afternoon in August 1932, Alec had done his day's work and, feeling the need for nourishment, closed up his shop and headed for Louie See Hing Lung's restaurant across the street.

Standing on the sidewalk in front of his shop, waiting for a horse-drawn-wagonload of hay to go by, he looked back at his shop window with deep satisfaction. There, lined up on a shelf, were eight pairs of half-soled leather boots to be picked up by their owners, as well as four pairs of unclaimed dress shoes on sale at very attractive prices ranging from $3.75 to $4.50. Alec Fook was used to people being unable to scrape together enough cash to reclaim their shoes.

Oh well, he thought. We are in a depression. Lots of men out of work. Who needs dress shoes when a man hasn't enough money to put food on the table? And the young ones still in school—what kind of future have they to look forward to?

He shook his head sadly, and his thoughts wandered to the mess that he heard was developing in Spain. Was that an omen of worse times to come?

The wagon passed by, its wooden, iron-rimmed, spoked wheels creaking, and since no more vehicles were forthcoming down Main Street, Alec Fook stepped off the wooden sidewalk in front of his shop and headed across the street, pleasant thoughts of the meal he would soon be consuming at the restaurant running through his mind.

He failed to notice two teenaged boys hiding behind a parked car in front of Jim brothers' store. But suddenly one of the boys emerged into the street with something coiled in one hand. It looked like a lasso cowboys used when chasing loose cattle across a field.

What does a boy want with a lasso on Main Street? Alec wondered.

The boy, now standing in the middle of the street, held the looped rope in his right hand, swinging it in widening circles over his head. As he neared Alec, he swung the loop forward.

Alec didn't have time to realize that the boy was going to lasso him until the noose passed over his head and shoulders, coming to rest on his chest just above his ample midsection. Dammed fool! Alec thought.

The boy tightened the rope and began to drag Alec, a few steps at a time, along the street. But Alec acted quickly, and in a split second, he loosened the rope encircling his chest with his left hand, getting enough slack to allow his right hand to draw his razor-sharp leather-cutting knife out of his vest pocket. The knife was spring-loaded, and when Alec pressed the button between a thumb and forefinger, the short shiny blade sprang forth. The boy tugging on the rope saw the blade flashing in the sunlight but didn't quite grasp what Alec was doing.

Alec, chuckling to himself, gripped the rope in his left hand

and cut it loose where it looped around his chest. Then, with the rest of the rope clutched in his left hand, he began a slow march toward his tormentor, cutting off chunks of rope as he went, smiling and inching toward the unsuspecting boy still tugging at the other end.

The tug of war didn't last long. The boy, seeing the knife flashing in Alec's hand and realizing that Alec was coming closer, dropped his end of the rope in terror and ran. His accomplice, from his hiding place behind a parked car, saw Alec advance like an avenging devil toward his friend, his knife blade flashing. He also panicked, and ran out to join his pal in full flight.

The two boys sprinted a block down the street and stopped, out of breath, quickly looking back to see if Alec was still following. But Alec wasn't moving. He was standing in the middle of the street, grinning over a large pile of severed chunks of rope.

He triumphantly waved his shiny knife blade in the air over his head and shouted," Hey, boys, you forgot your rope!"

Like with the snow boulder incident at See Hing Lung's grocery store the year before, nothing was said by an obviously informed populace to condemn the stupid actions of the two teenage hooligans. The parents of the boys should have at least punished their sons, but given the town's hostile racial climate, they obviously felt no remorse and failed to take any corrective parental action.

Years later, on a summer visit to Lillooet, I met and reminisced with my close friend, Russel Norton. I reminded him of the See Hing Lung snowball caper and the lassoing of the shoemaker Alec Fook, as well as the several episodes of adultery that even the children of Lillooet were aware of. (The town had a terrible record of venereal disease, including syphilis and gonorrhea.)

"Russ," I said finally, "maybe I am too harsh in my criticism of the Lillooet citizenry of that era. Maybe similar things were going on in all the other towns in British Columbia."

Russel nodded. "Yeah, maybe. But from what I've heard over the years, Lillooet was the worst!"

TEN

SATURDAY IN LILLOOET

It was a bright summer Saturday morning, June 12, 1932. Fourteen-year-old Ernie had decided to walk uptown from Grandpa Reynolds's house on Cayoosh Creek, where he had stayed overnight. He had a mission. He wanted to look at some boots in Jim brothers' store before he went home to the Bishop house on Main Street. The ones he was wearing had been re-soled twice, and Alec Fook, the town shoemaker, had warned him that he needed to buy a new pair because the stitching on the old pair was coming loose.

The shoemaker went on to say, in his Chinese/English accent in which Ls and Rs were interchangeable or omitted altogether, "Shoe be like pepoo'. Ol' shoe die. Stitchee no come loose on new shoe. Maybe Jim Blooda sto' got a good new shoe fo' you."

Ernie had some money from pitching hay down at the Dickey farm. He hoped he had enough. There had to be enough left over so he could buy new denim pants and a shirt to go with them.

He shouldered his backpack, which contained the two sandwiches Grandmother had made for him, his favourite: thick slices of homemade dill pickle between thickly buttered slices of her homemade bread, snugly wrapped in waxed paper. His grandfather had handed him a nickel to buy a bottle of pop in case he got thirsty before he came home from shopping.

They waved goodbye to him as they stood in their kitchen doorway. "Remember to be careful with the eggs in the bucket in your backpack. Don't break any," Grandma shouted, giving an extra wave. Ernie waved back and headed for the road leading to town.

He made his way up Station Hill, stopping to get a drink of ice-cold water from Tom Manson's iron water tank nestled against the bank. He walked past the PGE station, past the cemetery, and across the railroad tracks onto Main Street. As he walked, he wondered if he could find a pair of leather boots he could afford. He knew they would cost a lot more than running shoes, which went for two dollars. He had saved up six dollars all told.

There was, as usual on a weekend, a bit of traffic on the road: a few trucks with their shoulder-high, removable wooden slat guards; the occasional automobile; and three or four horse-drawn wagons, usually with an indigenous man and wife sitting on the wagon seat. In the back of the wagon there was always a bale of hay and a bag of oats. Sometimes a mid-sized dog would trail behind, brought along to stick by the unhitched wagon and unharnessed horses. Dogs would keep strangers away from the vehicles left parked in one of Lillooet's back alleys.

Lillooet, when I was a boy, was like a frontier town. Its back alleys were used as public parking lots and urinals for man and beast. The smell from the urine and manure—the horse piss and horse shit—was powerful and either very debilitating or very invigorating. You could stand and hold your nose to avoid debilitation—that was a sort of passive resistance—or you could move away as fast as your feet would carry you—that was invigorating, a sort of active resistance.

Tom Manson used to tell me, "Gordon, horse piss is good

for you, toughens up your lungs. And horse shit is good for the garden, gives you fruit and potatoes and vegetables."

I didn't believe that first part, so I usually stayed away from the Indian horses when they were tethered to someone's fence in the back alley. They scared me. As my Uncle Alvin from Big Bar used to say, "If you are going to work around horses, you're eventually going to get hurt. Count on it!"

Despite our fear, my friends and I used to hang around whenever a male horse, a stallion, indicated that it was about to urinate. It would spread its rear legs. Its penis would emerge from its loins and extend to a three-foot length under its belly, dangling menacingly over the ground. Finally it would release a stream of yellow urine which bored a hole six inches deep into the muddied soil.

As I write, the pungent smell of equine urine comes back to my olfactory sense. I do think that we adolescent boys secretly dreamed that our sex organs would someday mature and reach "stallion magnitude." I have to admit that I was fascinated by the spectacle, as were my pals. We waited and watched until the tremendous penis had shrunk its way back into its protective pouch and the stallion had returned to its quiet solitude, tethered to the back alley fence. In tribute, we appended a new phrase to our Rabelaisian vocabulary. Whenever, on a hike, when one of us needed to urinate very badly, he would shout, "Hang on, guys, I gotta piss like a racehorse!"

The same morning Ernie, unknown to me, was on his way up Main Street, I was in front of See Hing Lung's restaurant, watching the out-of-town folk gather to do their shopping at Parks' or Jim brothers'. I heard a noise, turned around, and saw Old Teciah approaching. Teciah was a friendly person, an elderly Fountain Valley Indian chief. He was a philosopher with a quaint command of the English language. One day, when I was with my dad in front of Parks' store, my dad stopped and talked with him. After a while he asked, "Teciah, why didn't you bring your wife with you today?"

Teciah shook his head sadly from side to side and replied, "Roop"—Dad's name was Reuben—"my wife, she been sick."

"That's too bad," said my dad. "How long has she been sick?"

"She been sick three days now," replied Teciah sadly. "Yesterday, today, and tomorrow."

On this day, Teciah must have come from the alley behind Jim Larter's smithy. That was where he usually unhitched his horse when he came to town. He and Mr. Larter were old acquaintances.

I smiled at Teciah, and he smiled back at me. He said he had just unhitched his wagon and tied up, fed, and watered his team. He took off his sombrero, and I watched as he dusted it off with a red handkerchief from his hip pocket.

"Teciah," I asked him, "Why do you Indians always carry hay in the backs of your wagons?"

With a wide grin, Teciah answered, "Cars burn gas. Horses burn hay. Cars give off smoke from their rear ends. Horses fart out of their assholes. Isn't that easy to figure out?"

I nodded in agreement. You couldn't outwit Teciah!

Meanwhile, back down on Main Street, Ernie walked along toward the centre of town. He was anxious to see what was for sale in Parks' store and Jim brothers' store, but he decided he would try Jim brothers' first, wondering if he had enough money to pay for the nice-looking leather Leckie boots he had seen on display in the back the week before. Running shoes were okay, but leather shoes looked more adult. He didn't want leather oxfords, not fancy dress shoes, but leather boots would be perfect.

As he pondered his dilemma, he approached Karl Lorentz's house. It was rather small, set twenty-five feet back from the sidewalk. Ernie admired it. Karl had built it himself, a nice piece of work with yellow cedar siding, a red-stained shingled roof, and a white-rimmed door frame and windowsills.

Karl looked up from where he was working at his woodpile beside the house. He put down his axe when he noticed Ernie and shouted, "Hey, Ernie, hold your horses. Have you got time for a chat?"

Karl wanted to talk fishing and pass on information about the steelhead run in the Thompson River near Lytton. Karl was an expert on steelhead. Ernie had heard about it and was getting interested in that sport. He was already very skilled at catching rainbow trout and Dolly Vardens, but he itched to try his hand at catching bigger fish, and Karl was the man to see.

It was reported in the *Bridge River Lillooet News* that the weekend before, Karl had caught a twenty-nine-inch steelie that weighed almost nine pounds. Karl caught it while fishing in the Thompson River. He'd used a salmon-egg spoon and cast into the huge pool just below Spence's Bridge. Since Lytton was forty-seven miles south of Lillooet, and Spence's Bridge was twenty-five miles further, Ernie had no hope of fishing in the Thompson. Neither he nor Karl had access to a car, but maybe they could arrange a ride with a member of the Lillooet Rod and Gun Club.

Karl never wore waders when he fished, Ernie likewise. They relied on their spin casting skills and fished from the bank. Ernie wore an old pair of running shoes when he fished in Cayoosh Creek. But he wanted a good pair of leather boots like Karl wore.

Karl used fresh or preserved salmon eggs as bait when fishing from the shore, and employed a simple short-bait casting technique. When he wanted to fish a big pool twenty feet offshore, he used a spoon hook, sometimes extra-baited with artificial salmon eggs as an incentive to get a big steelie to bite. That meant spin casting to drop the lure where you wanted it to go. Karl was an expert. And he didn't ever want to wade. If a person fell and his waders filled with water, it made getting up difficult and increased the likelihood of drowning. Karl wore leather boots.

Ernie showed Karl the boots he was wearing, and Karl agreed they had seen better days. He advised Ernie to get a good pair of leather boots and waterproof them with dubbin just in case he slipped and got them wet. He said waders were great for placer mining and fly fishing in quiet water but no good for steelhead fishing on a fast-flowing creek or river.

"Thanks for the info about the steelies," said Ernie. "Now I'd better hurry up and take these fresh eggs to Jim brothers' store." Nodding to Karl, he opened the gate of Karl's front yard and headed once again down Main Street. Karl waved goodbye as Ernie walked away.

Ernie said hello to Clara Jim as he entered Jim brothers' store. He opened his backpack and carefully put the bucket of Grandmother's eggs on the counter. Clara was minding the cash register and bagging and wrapping items for people as they paid and left. She quickly took the eggs and put them into the refrigerator. Then she went to the cash register and took out money to pay Ernie for the eggs.

There was no use asking Clara about boots. She knew nothing about shoes. Ernie would have to go by himself to the back of the store, find the shoes he was thinking of buying, take them out of their box on the shelf, and try them on. If he liked them, he could put them back in their box, with the price marked clearly on one end, and bring them to Clara at the cash register.

When he got to the back of the store, Don Jorgenson was trying on a pair of boots. They were Leckie's, the kind Ernie was interested in buying. He went over and said hello. "Those look like good boots, Don. Are they Leckie's?"

"Yep, they are," Don replied.

"I was thinking of buying a pair," Ernie went on, "if they have my size and if I can afford them."

"What size do you take?" asked Don.

"I take a ten," said Ernie.

"Same as me," said Don as he put the shoes back in their box. "They are a perfect fit, but just look at the price: eight seventy-five!"

Ernie looked at the end of the box and saw $8.75 on the price tag. He knew he could never afford more than $2.50, the price of a new pair of running shoes, not if he was going to get the denim shirt and pants he needed as well. *There's no use looking at boots you can't afford*, he murmured to himself.

Just then someone nudged his elbow. It was Georgie Pizzi. "Hi, Ernie. Karl Lorentz was telling me that you are interested in steelhead fishing. I'll be driving down to the Thompson River next Sunday. Maybe you and Karl should come with me. What do you think?"

Ernie was overjoyed and eagerly accepted the offer. He and Georgie moved to one side to begin a detailed conversation on steelhead technique.

But while he and Georgie Pizzi talked, Ernie was secretly watching what Don Jorgensen was up to. Don had taken down a second box, a box of running shoes priced at $2.50, and was quietly switching their contents, putting the expensive $8.75 boots into the cheap box and the cheap shoes into the expensive box.

Finally, glancing around once more for witnesses, Don quietly put both boxes back into their former places on the shelf. Of course, Ernie saw exactly where Don had placed the expensive box. The location was *fixed* in his mind.

When Don passed Ernie and Georgie, he stopped and said, "Nice seeing you both again. Like to stay and chat, but my wife is waiting in the hotel restaurant. See you around."

Ernie correctly guessed that Don Jorgensen wasn't going to meet his wife but would soon return after everyone had forgotten his presence in the shoe section in the back of the store and pick up the expensive Leckie boots for the paltry sum of $2.50.

So as soon a Don left the store, Ernie turned to Georgie and, pulling out his pocket watch, said, "Look at the time. Georgie, I have to go. I'll just have time to pick up a pair of boots and leave. Can I drop in on you on Wednesday after dinner? Maybe we could talk about next Sunday."

"Okay," said Georgie. "I'll see you on Wednesday."

Ernie went to the shelf where Don Jorgensen had placed the expensive Leckie boots, now hidden in their cheap running-shoe box.

Quietly, he took down the nefarious box and tucked it under his arm. Then he calmly strolled to the front of the store and handed Clara the box and the money. She looked at the price on the end of the box and innocently rang up $2.50 in the cash register.

She offered Ernie a paper bag to put the box into, but he politely declined her offer, murmured a hurried goodbye, and quietly left the store.

Outside, he ducked into the entrance to Wo Hing's store next door and calmly, covertly put the boxed expensive shoes out of sight into his rucksack. Breathless and happy, he shouldered his precious load and headed for home up Main Street. When he got home, he didn't show the shoes to the rest of the family. Someone was bound to ask how much he had paid for them—and where he had gotten the money. That was nobody's business but his own!

He met Don Jorgensen one Saturday two months later, on the street in front of Billy Taverna's barbershop. Don casually came up to Ernie and said in a low voice, "You SOB. You stole my Leckie leather boots right out from under my nose!"

Ernie replied, just as quietly, "Well, Don, I paid for them fair and square. The price was there, right on the end of the box."

ELEVEN
LILLOOET AND THE PGE RAILROAD BRIDGE

Once, Anderson Lake and Seton Lake were one long, prehistoric, unnamed lake, a glacial remnant stretching from the town of Darcy in the west to its eastern tip three and a half miles from Lillooet, a distance of approximately twenty-five miles.

But about twenty thousand years ago, a sudden landslide occurred halfway along that original long lake, dividing it into two separate lakes of approximately equal length. The western half is now known as Anderson Lake, and the eastern half is named Seton Lake.

The material from that huge landslide blockage is now the site of a town named, in the local Indian dialect, *Shalalth*. In English, it's Seton Portage.

Imagine that you, a modern canoeist, ignorant of the geological history of the region, intended to place your canoe into the water at Darcy, at the west end of Anderson Lake, and paddle the full twenty-five miles non-stop to the far eastern shore of Seton Lake, three and a half miles above the town of Lillooet. Well, halfway down Anderson Lake, you would suddenly come to know that your quest was impossible to achieve. You couldn't do it! You would encounter an insoluble problem after those first twelve and a half miles of paddling. Upon arriving at Shalalth, you would have to get out of your canoe, hoist it onto your back, struggle for a mile or so over the debris from that ancient landslide — making a portage, as the coureurs de bois would have described it — and then put your canoe back down into the water, this time into the west end of Seton Lake.

Then, if you paddled another twelve and a half miles east down Seton Lake, you would arrive at its east end, which is located on the west bank of the Fraser River.

Take thirty minutes or so when you reach the end of Seton Lake and paddle leisurely along the shoreline. Try to relax after your tiring canoe trip from Darcy, your portage at Shalalth, and that last stretch of paddling down beautiful, sky-blue Seton Lake. Take time to admire the setting. You would be sitting in a canoe on Seton lake between two huge mountains, Mount Brew to the south and Mount McLean to the north, both 8,500 feet above sea level. If you waited around until dusk, you'd be able tobserve the local mountain goats coming down over the top of each mountain onto the cliffs, to sleep safely out of reach of predators.

As you paddled across the end of the lake, you would have noticed the gap in the shoreline at the head of Seton Creek, through which the water of Seton Lake drains three and a half miles downstream into the Fraser River at Lillooet.

Wrong again!

You might even have imagined you could remain in your canoe and paddle those three and a half miles directly down Seton Creek to reach the town of Lillooet. But this, too, would soon prove to be impossible.

You would be able to travel just one short mile down Seton Creek, at which point you and your canoe would be confronted by an impassable one-thousand-foot-high nose of granite protruding southward out of Mount McLean and blocking Seton Creek entirely, forcing you to hang a right through a final two hundred yards of sky-blue Seton Creek until it disappeared, blending in with the glacier-green waters of Cayoosh Creek.

Seton Creek, as a separate entity, would have ceased to exist.

The two creeks, Seton and Cayoosh, now united in a forced marriage, would spend an abbreviated three miles of rough married life together, all downhill, before disappearing into the wide, deep, greedy, anonymous, muddy, placid Fraser River.

You could continue paddling downstream but only in the combined creek waters of Seton Creek and Cayoosh Creek, heading unwittingly toward the Fraser River two miles downstream and arriving at the mouth of Cayoosh Creek. You would, I hope, see the Fraser River looming up before you in good time and pull in to shore, thus ending your fruitless canoe trip in safety.

Looking up over your left shoulder from the beach, you would see the *town* of Lillooet, your intended target, on its elevated glacier flat one hundred feet above where you are standing beside your canoe. Your plan to paddle your canoe all the way to town has come to an unhappy end.

In 1912, when the Pacific Great Eastern Railway was conceived, its southern terminus was planned to be Squamish (another Indian word), and its northern terminus was to be Quesnel (a French word). The line was to pass directly through the town of Lillooet.

From Squamish, the route was to proceed through Pemberton, then the north side of Anderson Creek at an easy zero grade, on through Shalalth and the north side of Seton Lake, then continue down Seton Creek a further three and half miles directly to Lillooet. But Mother Nature had a surprise for the planners.

One mile down Seton Creek, the proposed right-of-way was, in fact, completely blocked by that thousand-foot-high nose of granite protruding out of Mount McLean behind Lillooet, directly into the creek's path.

Because the PGE, at this juncture, could not enter the town of Lillooet on the town flat one hundred feet above—the way the planners had blindly designed it—a temporary train station had to be set up on the south bank of Cayoosh Creek.

Merchants and travellers had to drive from the Main Street of Lillooet down the Station Hill road and over the Cayoosh Creek Bridge to get to the PGE depot. After the PGE freight for Lillooet was off-loaded from its cars, the train, in order to proceed to its final terminus at Quesnel, had to first cross the Fraser River. So a half-mile-long railroad bridge was constructed, spanning the Fraser.

It stretched from the west side, the lush Lillooet side, to the arid East Lillooet side with its sagebrush-covered flats. From here, the train could travel north up the east side of the Fraser River to the next stop, the small town of Clinton.

This was a stopgap measure that would have to be corrected later, because the original plan called for a roundhouse replete with switching yards and repair and maintenance facilities, as well as lubricant and fuel storage at Lillooet. The only suitable site was the uninhabited southern third of the town flat. There was definitely no room for such a project on Cayoosh Creek.

I'm not sure when the PGE civil engineering staff decided to solve the problem caused by the granite nose blockage. But I remember, as a three-year-old, being driven down the Station Hill road to watch the PGE come 'round the bend and stop at Cayoosh Creek Station.

So it was after 1928 when underground mining crews arrived on the scene and used TNT to blast a right of way through the granite nose, allowing the PGE to directly enter Lillooet. Cayoosh Station was abandoned, and the half-mile Fraser River bridge was soon replaced by a much shorter railway bridge that crossed the Fraser several miles north of the town, where an extremely narrow canyon compressed the river to a fraction of its width. A narrow canyon meant a shorter, cheaper bridge.

Seton Creek, of course, had to be left to its natural route, joining with Cayoosh Creek as it does to this day. And the PGE Railway could now run directly into Lillooet. Hooray for miners and TNT!

On the East Lillooet flats, workers removed the roadbed of iron rails and wooden ties and stripped the bridge of all possible fixtures, like the steel-and-wood substructure that had supported the wooden ties and rails. But its basic iron-and-wood upper frame was left intact and well posted with warning signs: "Unsafe For Human Traffic," "No Foot Passengers Allowed," etc.

However, the signage did not inhibit enterprising locals from improvising a walkway across the bridge, planking the gaps between the steel frames that rested on the concrete pillars still embedded in the river bottom. It was a suitable and safe route for foot traffic, provided one kept one's nerve and didn't look down at the fast-flowing river beneath one's feet. A misstep would result in a quick death by drowning in the muddy, ice-cold water below.

To a stranger unfamiliar with bridge construction, the bridge looked normal, intact, and ready for rail traffic. And so it remained until after World War II, when all the remnants were completely removed and the old Fraser River railway bridge was just a memory in the minds of a few Lillooet old-timers.

As a child, I was often allowed to walk with some friends to the Lillooet PGE station—just across the tracks from the Lillooet cemetery—to observe the weekly arrival of the PGE passenger-freight train from Vancouver, every Thursday night at eleven o'clock.

It was very exciting to be the first to spot the blinding headlight of the train, rounding the bend at Conway's farm, and to shout, "Here it comes!" We watched with anticipation as the engine coasted the last hundred yards, passing slowly in front of us eager onlookers standing on the platform.

The engineer would stop the train precisely to allow passengers to alight in front of the waiting crowd and be met by relatives, friends, or the local taxi driver. The freight cars, too, were exactly positioned to allow freight to be off-loaded quickly onto trucks or vans, which sped uptown to waiting storekeepers.

The postmaster, Mr. P. C. Wilson, collected his mail from the express car immediately behind the passenger car, and anyone expecting some kind of delivery from Vancouver had to wait for it to be handed over by the stationmaster himself in his office, which fronted on the platform behind us.

Then the train would begin to puff and slowly pull away from the station, picking up speed as it passed along the southern edge of town and headed for its next stop at Clinton, BC, population seven hundred souls.

The local joke about Clinton involved a group of American mining engineers, geologists, and gold mining investors sitting in the lobby of the Clinton Hotel, smoking and talking in loud tones about the big cities they had visited in Canada, the USA, and Europe. Back in a corner of the lobby sat old Jake Johnson, quietly chewing tobacco, listening in his usual chair next to the brass spittoon. Suddenly, Jake had had enough of this high falutin' big city talk! So he jumped up, walked over, confronted the tycoons, and shouted, "I'll have you fellers know that Clinton is no slouch of a town!" Then, turning his back to them, he stomped out into the night. Hooray for Jake Johnson!

A few benefits accrued from the abandonment of the Fraser River PGE bridge and the building of the new route right through the town. The first benefit to me personally was that the PGE tracks now passed right behind our back door, near where Tom Taylor, our close neighbour, stored his rail inspection handcart right against the bank.

Tom was a PGE track inspector. His job entailed a weekly daylight check of the rails, ties, spikes, and gravel roadbed, all the way from Lillooet to the newly constructed PGE bridge across the Fraser Canyon, several miles north. The railway provided Tom with a lightweight, manually operated, two-seater inspection handcar that he propelled by hand-pumping up the line and back every Saturday, from about ten in the morning until two in the afternoon.

If I was waiting for him down at the train tracks when he arrived, Tom would greet me with, "Good morning, Gordy. Would you like to go for a short ride and help me inspect some railroad tracks?"

I would, of course, reply, "Yessir!"

So he would unchain the padlocked handcart where it was parked on its wooden ramp ten feet from the tracks, wheel it down, and lift it up one end at a time onto the rails. After he had secured his food, Thermos, and extra rain gear in a small wooden compartment, I climbed onto the opposite seat facing him. He motioned for me to grasp my end of the two-handled pump arm, and, putting the handcart in gear, away we went, the two of us pumping, pumping, pumping along the railway. Of course, Tom was watching the roadbed as we travelled, but I concentrated on pumping. I was on cloud nine!

After three hundred yards, Tom nodded his head, our signal to stop pumping and for me to dismount. But first, Tom asked, "Well, Gordy, does the track look okay?"

I, of course, replied, "Everything is okay, sir!" and got down and stood back.

I waved to Tom as he moved off, and he waved back with his left hand while pumping with his right. Soon he was out of sight around the bend behind Webster's. I found the steps of the trail I had made on previous trips and climbed the bank, stooping carefully through the barbed wire to avoid tearing holes in my jacket. Then I stood up on the road and floated all the way home on *cloud ten*!

My two older brothers, Allan and Ernie, enjoyed another benefit of the movement of the PGE station: they began crossing the abandoned railroad bridge on the improvised plank walkway and, armed with twenty-two-calibre rifles, hunted the wild rabbits that proliferated on the East Lillooet sagebrush flats. (The East Lillooet flats were where the Canadian government established an internment camp for some of the Japanese-Canadians rounded up and transported away from the coast after the bombing of Pearl Harbour in December 1941.) Allan and Ernie came back from East Lillooet, each with three big rabbits and tales of the other creatures they had seen: coyotes, grouse, pheasants, gophers, bull snakes, and rattlesnakes.

I was curious about the snakes. "Aren't they poisonous?" I asked.

"Yes, rattlesnakes are lethal," Ernie answered, "but we don't have rattlesnakes on our side of the Fraser River. And we don't have bull snakes, either. So you don't have to worry about snakes."

Later I found out that bull snakes are members of the boa constrictor family. They can actually kill and eat rattlesnakes, so they must be immune to rattlesnake venom. They kill and eat rabbits too. They have special jaws that unhinge, allowing them to swallow large prey. Rattlesnakes prey mainly on the ubiquitous field mice living on the East Lillooet flats.

I must be part bull snake, because I remember how delicious fried rabbit was. We ate only the large hind legs, which tasted almost like fried chicken.

The PGE Railway brought an injection of life and a steady stream of fresh faces into our small world. Such was the nature of Lillooet life, however, that the railroad brought with it tragedy as well as excitement.

Lillooet had witnessed several incidents of suicide, murder, and drowning in the past, sometimes involving well-known members of the Lillooet community. But one afternoon in August 1937, the news went around that a recent visitor, a woman—a complete stranger—had walked out of her room in the Victoria Hotel on Main Street, down Station Hill, across Cayoosh Creek Bridge, and across the Indian Cayoosh Reservation before climbing out onto the abandoned railroad bridge. With her underclothing loaded with stones, she ended her life by jumping into the water. Did anyone actually see her jump? I wondered. How did they know she had loaded her underwear with stones? I never found out.

But that evening, my mother told my brother and me that she had seen that woman coming down Station Hill. "She looked so very, very sad. I'll never forget the look on her face. I wonder what drove her to take her own life."

Mount Brew and Mount MacLean's granite nose.

The original PGE railway bridge crossed the
Fraser River south of Lillooet.

New PGE railway bridge five miles north of Lillooet.

Old Highway bridge, closed in 1955.

Closeup of Old Highway bridge.

TWELVE
GIUSEPPE (JOE) PIZZI

"Datsa my egg-a you got in you basket!" shouted Mr. Pizzi, leaning on our back fence one Saturday morning. My brother Ernie, deliberately standing in plain view in our backyard, tipped forward so that Mr. Pizzi could see inside the basket of chicken eggs he was holding.

Joe Pizzi, as we all called him — really Giuseppe, or Joseph in Italian — had come from Italy in 1919 and settled into the Lillooet community where his cousin, Gino Santini, had come before the First World War. Joe spoke broken English with a strong accent that added an *a*, *o*, *i*, or *e* sound to the end of most words. Because most Italian words end in a vowel, Italian is a lovely language for opera. I think it is the most beautiful-sounding language of all.

The night before, my brother Ernie had secretly sneaked two dozen eggs into our kitchen from our grandmother's chicken farm on the Cayoosh flats, where she raised six hundred laying hens. Early the next morning, he waited until Mr. Pizzi was up and out in his own backyard and, at the right moment, he came out of the barn and shouted to Mr. Pizzi, "Look how many eggs I found in our barn this morning."

"Datsa not you egg-a," shouted Mr. Pizzi, leaning heavily on our fence. "Datsa my egg-a!"

No, no, Mr. Pizzi," replied Ernie. "Those eggs were laid in our barn, and anything we find in our barn belongs to us. I check each day, Mr. Pizzi, and I get a lot of fresh eggs."

"But you gotta no chickie," said Mr. Pizzi angrily. "How canna you get egg-a when you gotta no chickie? Datsa my egg-a! My chickie, he lay egg-a in you barn-a."

"Well," Ernie asked, "What are your chickens doing in our barn? Why don't they stay in their own yard? You have a big yard."

"Chickie like to look-a for food, datsa what chickie do," shouted Mr. Pizzi. "Chickie like to eat-a da bug."

"Yeah," said Ernie. "They come into our yard, looking for bugs, because you let them, and we are tired of stepping in the shit from your chickens. You should keep your chickens in your own yard. Look at our good strong picket fence. It was built to keep out cows and horses, not chickens. Chickens can squeeze right through the pickets. Why don't you pen your chickens up? You let them wander everywhere, and they come into our yard and shit all over the place. Maybe you don't give your chickens enough to eat. Maybe they get hungry and come over into our backyard, looking for grasshoppers, and when the chickens get full of our grasshoppers, they have to go poo-poo."

"Why donna you fix-a you fence-a?" Mr. Pizzi retorted, "so my chickie never can-a come to you place?"

"If you don't want to fence in your chickens," said Ernie, "you can tell your rooster, since he's the boss of your chickens, that the Whitney family is going to throw lots of wheat on the ground for your hens to come over and eat. And tell him we are going to build nice nest boxes in our barn for them to lay their eggs in. We've got lots of room. And we can sell any eggs we don't eat to Jim Brothers' store. One family can only eat so many eggs, you know. Look how many eggs I got in my basket this morning!"

Mr. Pizzi looked stunned, and all he could say, as he retreated from our fence, was, "Datsa my egg-a you got in you basket!"

Ernie grinned at Mr. Pizzi's retreating back, and went, smiling, through our back kitchen door—after checking his boots for chicken shit.

Later that day, we could hear sounds of carpentry coming from Joe Pizzi's chicken yard. He was at last penning up his chickens properly, so they couldn't lay eggs in *da neighbour's yarda*. The die had been cast. My clever brother had won the battle, and there was no more *Pizzi chickie shit-a* in our yard.

Now that the Pizzis' chickens were properly penned, I think Ernie really missed goading Joe Pizzi's big, scrappy Rhode Island Red rooster into a fighting mood. It used to fly furiously at Ernie whenever he leaned over the fence and crowed. Ernie was a good mimic. He could imitate a rooster crowing, a cow mooing, a horse neighing, a goat or sheep bleating, even a motorcycle starting up and roaring off down the road. Now that the Pizzis' chickens were properly penned, there was no more rooster goading for Ernie to enjoy. On the other hand, there was no more smelly chicken shit for us to scrape off our shoes before going into the house.

Ernie had a low opinion of Mr. Pizzi. It was obvious to me after the argument over the toilet habits of Mr. Pizzi's peripatetic chicken flock, but my brother may have had other reasons not to treat him with the respect usually due to one's elders.

Two years before, he and my brother Allan were getting their beer bottle collection ready to take to the junk dealer when I heard Ernie say, "Guess what I saw last Saturday."

"Gimme a clue," said Allan.

"Well," said Ernie, "you know Maggie Pete, don't you?"

"She's the mother of Raymond, Bessie and Beulah Rebagliatti."

"*Was* their mother, you mean," said Ernie. "Their father kicked her out because she was sleeping with other men. She was cheating on her own husband."

"A lot of men in Lillooet cheat on their wives too," Allan retorted. "What has that to do with Joe Pizzi?"

"Wait 'til you hear this!" Ernie went on. "Last summer, I was chasing grasshoppers in our yard for fishing bait when Mr. Pizzi came out his back door with Maggie Pete in tow. I watched them go into his small tool shed behind his house and close the door behind them. I thought maybe she wanted to borrow a pair of grass shears, but about twenty minutes later, I saw Joe Pizzi come out of his shed all alone, with no Maggie Pete behind him."

"So he must have left her alone in the shed," Allan said. "What would Maggie Pete be doing all by herself in Joe's tool shed?"

"Maybe she was putting her clothes back on," said Ernie, grinning.

"Why would she have taken her clothes off?" Allan said with a puzzled look on his face.

He was really naïve about sex, I guess.

"Well," said Ernie, laughing, "Mr. Pizzi came out of the shed, chuckling aloud to himself, and said, 'I no think she do, but-a she do!' Do I have to draw you a picture?"

Allan laughed. "You mean he was screwing her in his own tool shed, and with his own tool!"

"Isn't that what a tool shed is for?" Ernie smirked, and the two of them broke into hysterical laughter. Mrs. Pizzi must have heard their outburst, because she looked out her kitchen window.

Later on, one of my chums confirmed—and elaborated upon—Allan's assessment. But I wasn't convinced I knew what "screwing" was all about. I guessed all older men did the same as Mr. Pizzi, and I put it out of my mind.

Ernie may not have been Joe Pizzi's biggest fan, but as I grew older, I became friends with Joe and his wife, Luisa. They were both very fond of children. Their own four children had grown up, and all but one had moved away. The remaining daughter had three children, who were only a bit younger than me, and Joe and Luisa really enjoyed their company. So I was always welcomed when I knocked on the Pizzi door and asked, "May I please pick up some wind-fallen apples from under your water core apple tree?"

My teacher, Miss Edgecombe, had told me that the water core apple was actually harmlessly diseased. As it ripened, it stored so much sugar and water around its core, it couldn't be shipped to market. Eating one was like biting into honey. We children loved them. It was like candy to me. And whenever we begged for water core apples, Mr. Pizzi happily obliged.

"Shoo-a you can," replied Mr. Pizzi. "You take all-a you want. Take some to you mama. She can make you nice-a apple pie."

Joe Pizzi was an outstanding and resourceful gardener. His front yard, which faced right on Main Street, was a sight to behold. It was filled with flowers, mainly roses and sweet-smelling carnations, but one edge also contained a water core apple tree, a peach tree, a lilac tree, and a strange crabapple tree that bore large purple fruit with white powdery flesh. I tried many times to eat one but couldn't. (Maybe it was a diseased variety too.)

One of Mr. Pizzi's secrets was to use natural fertilizer. Every Sunday morning in the spring, you could spot Joe with his wheelbarrow and shovel, wheeling down the back alleys where the local Indians had tethered their horses overnight. He gathered load after load of horse manure. He would store it in his large backyard to ripen before spreading it gently around his flower beds and tree trunks.

Another project of Joe's was to build tiers into the sandy hillside at the back of his property. He realized that since it faced south and received much sunlight, it would make a fine terraced vineyard. He ameliorated the sandiness of the soil by burying in the terraces all the cotton rags he could collect from neighbours. A final layer of leaves and horse manure created a good loamy soil, and within a year, Joe had the beginnings of a fine vineyard. He became famous in Lillooet for the Christmas wine festival he hosted in his own home.

I often saw Joe Pizzi in my frequent wanderings on the outskirts of Lillooet because he worked as a grader for the Department of Public Works, levelling off the gravel verges of the town's roadways. I don't know how many years he held this job. I should have asked Jim Larter, the blacksmith, who often repaired the steel grader blades for the Works department.

Joe was a resourceful scrounger. When my uncle Ed Whitney returned to the USA from Lillooet in 1935, he left behind several vintage automobiles in his backyard. Nobody wanted them, so Joe Pizzi got Ed's permission to strip the cars of all their wiring. I wonder what Joe did with all that loot. He was a busy worker bee.

Later, one summer after I became a high school teacher, I took my wife Joanne back to Lillooet. We dropped in on Joe Pizzi late one afternoon. He remembered me as a child and took us out and around his front garden. All the passersby on Main Street used to stop and admire his beautiful roses, his apple and peach trees, his red carnation flower beds, the beautiful lilac tree, the profusion of flower beds containing marigolds, pansies, ox-eye daisies, lupines, snapdragons… You name it, Joe Pizzi had it in his front yard.

We three went back into his parlour, looked through several of his photo albums, and admired the Italian landscape paintings on the walls. As we were getting up to leave, Joe touched my shoulder and said, "Let me show you something I not show to everybody."

So we sat down as he retrieved from a cabinet a paper box as long as my forearm and placed it on the table in front of us. He carefully opened the box and removed a beautiful silk necktie. With tears in his eyes, he explained that Luisa had given him this tie on their wedding day in Italy. He said he had never worn it since he'd come to Canada. There were tears in Joanne's eyes, too, as Joe returned the box to its cabinet sarcophagus.

Years later, I asked Tom Manson if he remembered Joe Pizzi. Joe would have been around eighty then. "Of course," he replied. "Joe Pizzi was one of Lillooet's pioneers. He came to Canada from Italy about the time the First World War ended, the same time as Dr. Stewart came to Lillooet from England. Joe was a wonderful gardener, and he made a nice dry white wine from the grapes he grew in those terraces behind the Bishop House, where you used to live.

"Can you imagine," Tom went on, "turning a barren, sandy, sagebrush hillside into a beautiful vineyard? I drank many a glass of Joe's wine at his Christmas parties. I think there were thirty people there. A few got drunk. Shorty was one of them."

"Did Joe Pizzi die in the Lytton Hospital like Shorty Laidlaw did?"

"No," said Tom. "Joe Pizzi spent the last year of his life in a rest home in Victoria. He was eighty-one when he died at Victoria Jubilee Hospital. Joe and Luisa lie buried side by side in our Lillooet cemetery. You should go see their graves if you have time."

"We have time," I said, "and we will do so today before we head back to Vancouver." We entered the cemetery on our way out to the highway and found their gravesites in the directory.

I must confess that tears came to my eyes as we stood before their two headstones. I murmured to myself, "Rest in peace, Giuseppe. Rest in peace, Luisa."

Joanne and Gordon honeymooning in Lillooet, 1954.

Joanne visiting Joe Pizzi's flower garden, 1980.

THIRTEEN
FRANK GOTT

On the drive from Squamish to Lillooet through the upper
Cayoosh Creek Canyon, the road passes Gott Creek. This
name always jogs my memory, and an image appears in my
mind of a tall, slender, sixty-year-old, part-indigenous man — a
"half-breed," as the locals would say — wearing his usual
Canadian Army cap with its regimental badge pinned above its
visor.

His name was Frank Gott, and he was a Lillooet war hero
to us boys because he had been in the army, in France, during
the Great War. Whenever my friends and I played Cowboys
and Indians or Soldiers, I used to think of Frank Gott and his
skill with a rifle. He was a crack shot. I heard that he had been
a sniper in the Canadian infantry and had killed many German
soldiers on the front line. I heard too that once, using his army
rifle with a telescopic sight, Frank Gott had stood in Artie
Phair's backyard and shot and killed a rabid dog across the
Fraser River — a distance of a thousand yards. We all knew
that Frank Gott was a close friend of Artie, the unofficial
mayor of Lillooet. (Lillooet, at this time, had not yet become a
municipality, so we didn't have a real mayor.) Every
Christmas, Artie gave Frank a brand-new army jacket and

army cap with a shiny badge to go with it. Frank Gott was one of my heroes.

When I was six years old, I used to play in the front yard of the Dillon family house with their three children. I remember the names: Don, Norton, and Leonard. Norton was my age and, at that time, my constant playmate. It was Norton who had alerted me, on Friday after school, that Frank Gott would be visiting their parents again on the Saturday morning. "It's a good chance," Norton said, "to ask Mr. Gott to eat a big male carpenter ant."

I was aghast. "Does he really eat ants?"

"Sure he does," said Norton. "All we have to do is catch a big one. I know where there is a rotten tree stump full of them."

Come Saturday morning, Mr. Gott, after his visit with Norton's parents, was just about to leave the Dillons' front yard when Norton asked him, "Mr. Gott, will you eat a big ant for Gordon? He's never seen you eat one."

"Of course," said Frank, with a big grin on his face. "Have you got an ant for me to eat?" Norton handed him a matchbox with an ant inside. Frank Gott carefully opened the box and took out the big carpenter ant. He handed back the empty box to Norton, popped the ant into his mouth, chewed on it, and swallowed it with gusto. I was in shock. My whole body shuddered.

"See?" said Norton, "What did I tell you?"

"That tasted really good, Norton," said Mr. Gott. "One of the best I ever ate! Thank you."

Later, when I told my mother about it, she laughed and said, "Frank Gott doesn't really eat ants. He palms the ants using sleight of hand like a magician does on stage." I didn't know what "palmed" meant, and I had never seen a magician on a stage. To this day, I still believe that Frank Gott ate the ant. Why not? Some people eat grasshoppers, locusts. Some people even eat frogs' legs.

A year later, I was walking down Main Street with another of my playmates, Johnny Wing. At the Victoria Hotel, we came upon a crowd of people milling around the back of a truck parked in front of the police station. We were moving toward the crowd when Georgie Pizzi, Joe Pizzi's son, stopped us. "Don't go any closer," he said. "You'd better not see this."

As we turned back toward my house at the upper end of Main Street, Tom Manson came out of the crowd and led Johnny and me back up the street. He sat down with us on the green bench in front of Billy Taverna's barbershop. "Frank Gott," he said, "has been killed in an accident. That's his body in the back of Artie Phair's truck. I don't want you to see it, there's a lot of blood there. They are going to take his body into the morgue inside the police station. You'd better go home. Your father and mother can tell you all about it later."

Well, I heard about it the next day, not from my parents — who were equally puzzled — but from Johnny Wing's older brother, Kay. Kay was furious. "Those bastards, those bastards! They didn't have to kill Frank Gott. Frank should have been taken to Kamloops to appear in court. He should have been put on trial, not shot down like a dog."

Even then, I didn't hear *all* about it until a month had passed and Tom Manson told me the sad story. "Frank Gott used to shoot deer out of season. He was breaking the law, true, but his ancestors, the Lillooet Indians, had killed deer for food all year round, long before the white men came to BC. And the country was full of deer. Bert Ferry, the new provincial game warden, warned Frank Gott verbally, on the street in Lillooet, to stop killing deer out of season. Was it once or was it twice, or was it more times? And had he actually caught Frank in the act? No, he had not! But what would his superiors in Victoria have said? Derelict in duty? No, it was only hearsay the game warden was going on, but he believed his sources to be reliable. So he felt he had to act."

"Bert Ferry decided to catch Frank Gott in the act," Tom

went on. "And, after several failed attempts, he managed to catch Frank Gott in the Yalakom Valley with a freshly killed deer on his pack horse. He hadn't seen Frank actually shoot the deer, but he knew that if he could examine the pack horse, he would find a dead deer. And he would have a witness as well, because Frank was with a companion, a teenage Indian boy. Bert Ferry said, 'Frank, I have to examine your pack saddle.' Frank Gott replied from the other side of the pack horse, 'One more step, Ferry, and I'll kill you.'

"Bert Ferry took the 'one more step,' and Frank Gott lifted his rifle and shot him dead, right between the eyes. Of course, the frightened teenage boy fled to his home and told his parents what had happened."

"Both parents were shocked. They felt drained and absolutely helpless, and yet they knew they had no choice but to report to the police what had happened."

"They did so, despite the knowledge that Frank Gott had killed that deer in order to provide food for them and their hungry children. When the townsfolk heard the boy's story, the police constable enlisted an armed volunteer posse that included Frank Gott's admirer, Artie Phair. The posse tracked Frank down within twenty-four hours," Tom said. "Frank resisted arrest, galloped off on his mount, and was shot off his horse, mortally wounded and bleeding profusely from multiple gunshot wounds."

So the town had to hold two funerals that week. Frank Gott was a Catholic. Bert Ferry was a United Church member. Frank was buried in the Catholic cemetery located up on the Indian reservation. Bert Ferry's body was interred in Vancouver.

I mourned for Frank Gott, even though I knew he broke the "white man's law." Even then, at six years of age, I felt our game laws did not dispense justice to Indian people. I thought that Bert Ferry should have allowed Frank Got to kill deer in secret, as long as our townspeople were kept in the dark. Then Bert Ferry's job would not have been threatened.

Had I been game warden in Bert Ferry's boots, perhaps I would have tried to arrest Frank Gott for violating the game law. But more than likely, I would have consulted George James, chief of the Lillooet Indian tribe, in the hope that tribal justice could prevail by putting sanctions on Frank Gott and thereby restraining his hunting activities.

Was I simply behaving childishly, hoping that somehow a solution could be found whereby Frank could continue in secret to harvest deer while the onus of enforcing the game law would never fall on Bert Ferry's shoulders? What would you have done?

Even as a child, I was angry at Artie Phair, at the irony wherein he, Frank Gott's friend and admirer, had taken up arms against him. To add to the irony, let me remind us all that Frank Gott was a war hero, a decorated army veteran of World War I.

Judge Begbie's hanging tree, upper town flats.

FOURTEEN

AN UNFORTUNATE DEATH

It was six o'clock Sunday morning in the sleepy little town, and I was already awake. I was one of Lillooet's earliest risers. I had to be, to be the first to pick up the empty bottles left behind by Saturday night's revellers.

The only other person who was astir this morning at such an early hour was Neve, the Pizzis' youngest daughter. Neve was out walking her dog, a small wire-haired terrier she called Riki. The energetic little dog was actually pulling Neve along the wooden sidewalk of Main Street as the two of them approached me.

I had just emerged from Egan's Alley, leaving one of my most lucrative spots for collecting empty whisky bottles: the Anglican minister's garbage can just outside the front gate. As I turned and looked up the street, I spotted Neve coming toward me, with little Riki tugging at his leash.

"Hey, Gordie," Neve greeted me. "You're up real early, aren't you?"

I nodded, patting Riki's curly head, and pointed to the gunny sack at my feet on the sidewalk.

"So," she said, smiling at me, "you've been busy collecting bottles, haven't you?"

I grinned as I tapped the neck of a bottle sticking out of my gunny sack. "Yes, I always get a lot of beer bottles from Egan's Alley. Fifteen cents a dozen, and I've already found eight beer bottles."

Neve chuckled. She knew the drinking habits of the Reverend Kaye, whose house was at the top of Egan's Alley— and he wasn't a beer drinker. "What will you do, Gordie, with all the money you make?"

"I'm saving up for a BB gun," I said. "I've seen a nice one in the Eaton's catalogue. It comes with a thousand BBs, too."

"You be careful with that BB gun," said Neve. "Don't point it at anybody or anything that's alive. Just aim at targets. You could put someone's eye out, so make sure you don't put the cans on a fence rail, like I saw you do last time. Put them on the ground. Promise me you will!"

"I promise I will. My brothers and I practise shooting at empty milk cans propped up against the clay bank in our backyard. I'm not a very good shot, but my brother Allan is, and Ernie, he's the champ!"

"Well, that's good," said Neve. "Now, Riki is getting restless. I take him for a long walk down Main Street before the stores open. Some people don't like to see dogs on the street."

"I know," I said. "I had the same problem when I had my dog, Fritz. You remember Fritz, don't you? Now I have only a cat, Woody, and he sticks around our house all day long. Maybe he wanders down Main Street at night."

Neve broke out with a loud laugh. "You have quite a strange sense of humour, Gordie, but then maybe cats do wander all over town at night."

I waved goodbye to Neve and Riki, cut across Main Street in front of Blanche Vinal's house, then went down the Dips and up the other side into my own front yard. I carefully emptied my gunny sack of whisky bottles behind the house and added them to the small stack piled against the wall. I stood back, happy, as I thought, "I'll soon have that BB gun."

My mother was waiting to cook me my breakfast of Quaker oatmeal porridge topped with Pacific condensed milk, a little water, and brown sugar. When I was finished, she set a plate with two slices of homemade bread in front of me. "Thanks, Mom." I smiled at her as I reached for the can of Roger's golden syrup. You couldn't buy bread in a store or bakery that tasted as good as my mother's. She poured me a cup of tea from the brown teapot. She said that I was too young for coffee, but maybe next year, after I was fully grown, I could have coffee.

"I wish I had something fun to do this morning, Mom, but most of my friends are still in bed," I said.

"Well, Tom Taylor said you can pick some of his transparent apples," my mother reminded me. "You know, those wonderful transparent apples from the tree near their back fence. Why don't you check them out?"

"Yes," I replied, "They should be ready about now." Tom Taylor, the PGE Railway track inspector, was always good to me.

"Just try not to make any noise opening their gate," my mother warned me. "You don't want to wake up Mrs. Taylor. We heard that she is not well."

"I'll be as quiet as a mouse," I said. "Shall I take the large pail by the kitchen door?" My mother nodded and, placing her finger to her lips, said, "Don't make any noise."

Very quietly, I closed our gate and headed for Tom Taylor's place a block away. His place was right on Main Street next to the Catholic church. As I passed, I could see smoke coming from some of the neighbours' chimneys. Most people would still be abed, I thought, but maybe a few were getting ready to go to early mass.

I was surprised, as I neared the Taylor's backyard, to see a stranger leaning against the fence with his back to me. He was looking up at the transparent apple tree. I stopped. What was the man doing this early in the morning? He wasn't after apples, was he?

No, he wasn't after apples, I realized. Something was wrong because the man — it was definitely a man — was just standing there, leaning, not moving a muscle.

I became frightened. I crept forward to get a closer look. I could see that the man was slumped against the fence, his knees buckled. Each of his hands clutched a sharp fence picket, and the pickets were squeezing his neck and face. The pickets were choking him to death!

I didn't know that the man had been dead for several hours as I yelled at the top of my voice, "Help, help! Somebody, come help!"

Nobody came, and, in a panic, I decided to go on my own to the policeman's office on Main Street and ask the constable to come help the man hanging on the picket fence.

I cut through the open churchyard to Main Street and ran for the police station. I had to pass the Pizzis' front yard, where Neve was out on the front lawn, tossing a ball for Riki to retrieve. She saw me running and shouted, "Hey, Gordie, stop! Stop!"

I stopped, panting, completely out of breath.

She could read the panic on my face. "What's wrong, Gordie?" she asked. "Why are you running? Where are you going?"

I quickly told her about the man hanging on Tom Taylor's fence. She could see I wasn't making it up, so she took me into their kitchen, sat me down, and phoned the police office.

Then Neve put her arms around my shoulders and said, "Someone should go over to the Taylor house and tell Mr. Taylor what you saw. Do you feel up to going with me?"

"Sure," I said. "I'll go with you. I'm not afraid now."

So Neve and I ran over and knocked on Tom Taylor's front door. Neve told Tom what had happened. Tom rushed around to his back fence just as the police car arrived. Then Doc Stewart came in Chuck Hurley's taxi and examined the body.

Tom Taylor came back to his front door fifteen minutes later and talked to Neve and me. "The dead man is Johnny Adolf, from the Fountain Valley reservation." He sadly shook his head. "He's been dead for over three hours according to Doc Stewart. It looks like he got drunk on too much logana wine at a party in Roy Doherty's house, just down the alley from here. He got sick and headed outside to throw up. He grabbed onto my back fence to steady himself, leaned forward, lost his footing, got his neck caught between the two pickets, and choked to death."

Neve took me back to her place, sat me down near the kitchen stove, and made me sip a glass of warm, diluted homemade wine. Her parents, Giuseppe and Luisa, were out on their front lawn, leaning over the fence and looking up and down Main Street, but there was nothing to see. The body of Johnny Adolf had been taken away after being disentangled from Tom Taylor's fence, placed in the back of Jim Larter's truck, wrapped in a blanket, and taken to the police station, which was used as a morgue when needed. Lillooet had no hospital and nothing close to a proper morgue.

"Would you like to see some baby chicks?" Neve asked. "We have two hens with thirty chicks between them. They are so cute and so pretty."

"Yes, yes, let's go and look them over," I replied with enthusiasm.

When we had seen all the baby chicks, I reminded Neve that my mother wouldn't know where I was. "Maybe she's worried. I should go home, so she can see I'm okay. I can tell her what happened."

"Yes, she will be worried," Neve replied, "and you can tell her all about the accident."

"Just imagine, Neve," I said. "I left my mother to go pick

transparent apples in Tom Taylor's yard, and this terrible thing happened, and I didn't get even one apple to take home."

"Well, Gordie, my brave little friend," Neve cooed with her face next to mine, "Don't you worry. You can take home some of our sweet water core apples. I'll get you a bag!"

"I don't need a bag, Neve. I still have the pail I bought from home. It's sitting on your back porch, remember?"

"Yes, you are right." Neve smiled. "We'll fill your pail with apples."

Neve Pizzi (top) with her schoolmates, 1930.

FIFTEEN
MRS. WING, NATUROPATH

"I'm bleeding, I'm bleeding! Run! Go get Mrs. Wing!"

It was midmorning in July 1933. The words came from the tent house in which my mother, unknown to me at that moment, was lying on a blood-soaked sheet on a bed in the temporary accommodation where she and my father slept.

We had just moved back to Lillooet after our stint in Gold Bridge. This time my father had been offered a job building a house on a subdivided lot in town. The owner of the half lot, a Mr. Wo Hing, (we called him "young" Wo Hing, because his father was known as "old" Wo Hing) had promised a lower-than-usual fee for building but free rent in perpetuity. My father sent a detailed plan for the building and asked the owner to have a portion of the lot bulldozed to the correct size for the foundation to be poured into place.

We pitched two tents on a corner of the bulldozed, levelled ground. We moved our belongings — beds, table, stove, etc. — into the two tents. In other words, we camped out there for one month while my father quickly framed the house, shingled the roof and the exterior walls, put in windows and doors, and panelled the interior walls with six-inch-wide, v-joint cedar.

I was eight years old, and I had already gotten out of my sleeping bag in my small pup tent and made my own breakfast in the cook tent, using our portable Coleman camp stove to boil the water.

My mother's scream galvanized me. I put my porridge bowl on the folding table outside my tent, ran to the tent house door, and peeked in. I saw my mother lying on her bed, her voice weakening as she said, "Hurry, oh hurry. Get Mrs Wing. Oh, hurry!"

"I'm going. I'm going, Mom," I shouted. "I'm going to get her!" My mother moaned her assent.

I sped through the gate, down the Dips, and up the other side, running with my heart in my mouth across the back alley, through the gate, and onto the Wing family's front porch. I pounded on their front door. Katy Wing and her sister Jessie Wing opened the door as I blurted out, "Come quick. My Mom's bleeding to death."

"Oh my God," screamed Katy. "Nina's having a miscarriage. Get the stretcher, Jessie, and follow me. Be quick! Be quick! Nina's hemorrhaging."

I ran back across the alley, down the Dips, up the other side, through the gate, and up to the flap of my mother's tent, with Katy and Jessie close behind.

In a flash, pushing me to one side, they lifted my mother onto the stretcher and carefully, tenderly, quickly, carried her sagging body across the Dips, across the back alley, and into the Wing family's living room.

Mrs. Wing, their mother, was awaiting their return and immediately took charge. She had already placed a rubber sheet and bedding on a single bed that had been pulled into the living room.

She said quietly to the two girls, "Lift her gently off the stretcher and onto the bed. Put a pillow under her head, and put these two stiff pillows under her knees, plus two more under her feet. We've got to keep her feet raised to stop the bleeding." Then she said, "Jessie, get my medical bag and find some clean cotton rags, some Kotex, for padding. We've got to pack cloths into her vagina and keep pressure on her cervix."

Then she called her younger daughter, Lily, from her bedroom. "Take young Gordie away into the restaurant," she said quietly, "and look after him!"

Needless to say, I was in a panic, and as Lily led me away, I burst into tears. "I don't want my mother to die."

Lily said soothingly, "Go ahead and cry, but your mother is not going to die. My mother won't let her die. She knows exactly what to do. But it's okay. If you have to cry, go ahead and cry."

So I cried as she put her arm around my shoulder and led me into the kitchen of the Wing family restaurant. She sat me down near the hot, oversized kitchen range.

After Lily had calmed me down a bit, she made me drink a mug of warm tea mixed with sugar and canned milk. I held both hands around its warmth as Lily quietly recounted what they were doing to look after my mother. "My mom knows exactly what to do. She has done this before, and she taught us girls how to do it too. Your mother will be okay now.

"Don't you remember," she went on, "that time you cut your hand with your jackknife? Didn't your mother put a tight bandage on the cut to stop the bleeding? That all happened on the outside of your body. Well, your mother's bleeding is inside her body, and the bleeding is being stopped by the bandages Katy and Jessie and my mother have put inside your mother's birth canal. I know you don't really understand what I am saying, but trust me, Gordie. When you're grown up, you'll understand."

I kept my eyes, full of hope, on her face. I began to believe her every word. I knew I had to.

"But don't you worry about your mother. Even now,

because her feet have been raised up on pillows, her body is starting to get better. The bleeding inside her body will soon stop, and her strength will come back. Remember how the blood on your cut finger stopped and hardened, and your finger got better? Well, your mother's body will start to heal as soon as her blood begins to clot and harden."

I must have had a puzzled look on my face, but Lily's confidence calmed me. I really didn't understand many of the words she used, but I believed her implicitly.

"It's a bit like a leaking garden hose," she continued. "When the hose springs a leak, such as when you are watering the lawn, you put your thumb on the hole, don't you? That's pressure, like the tight bandage on your cut finger. And you keep holding the pressure on the hole until someone shuts off the water. That's easy with a garden hose. With your mother, it's harder, but the idea is the same, and everything good is happening inside her body. And don't you forget that my mother is a doctor—not like Doc Stewart, but she is still a doctor. Now, come on," said Lily, "and drink your tea."

Mrs. Wing was, to us in the poorer class, a miracle worker. Lillooet had no hospital, and the nearest one was Lytton Hospital, forty-seven miles south on the Fraser Canyon Highway. Mrs. Wing was a first responder to poor whites, "half breeds," and indigenous tribal members, none of whom were anxious to go to Dr. Ployart, an employee of the provincial government. Their first choice was Mrs. Wing, whose expertise and social class endeared her to the Lillooet hoi polloi.

Mrs. Wing herself was shunned by the pioneer families in Lillooet—those who called themselves the "upper crust," a phrase I well understood, or the "Lillooet 400s," a phrase I never understood. The very well-to-do in Lillooet were always transported by private car, taxi, or postal service stage—stagecoach—one hundred miles east to Kamloops for hospitalization. Of course, this was after referral by Dr. Ployart, himself a member of the upper crust.

Mrs. Wing, unknown to the provincial government, was the medical caregiver to the poor, ninety percent of the Lillooet population, free of charge.

For Mrs. Wing "there oughtta be a medal," said Tom Manson. She was, in my opinion, the equal of our remittance man, our British medically trained man, Doc Stewart, who was probably once qualified, but who had been exiled from his native England. What crime was he guilty of? Incompetent surgery? Incest? Alcoholism? Gambling? He was called a remittance man because he received a monthly remittance from a bank in England. These funds were no secret, probably because the gossip mongers in Lillooet had access to all information concerning any citizen receiving mail from BC, Canada, or the world. Their source was the postmaster, Mr. Pat Wilson.

Nobody in Lillooet knew why Doc Stewart had been exiled. But I heard he was simply not certified for hospital surgery like Dr. Ployart. But the doc was allowed to practise medicine in Lillooet in a certain capacity, examining male recipients of relief funds to determine their competency or incompetency to do public works and earn their relief through ditch digging, road-gang labour, or snow clearance.

I presume Mrs. Wing and Doc Stewart met often to discuss the health of patients and the prevalent diseases of Lillooet's lower class. Syphilis and gonorrhea were common diseases in Lillooet, but I wasn't aware of Doc Stewart or Mrs. Wing being involved in related therapies. Lily Wing told me that Doc Stewart often called Mrs. Wing in to take over a patient in a nursing capacity because he did not have a decent venue and most likely didn't possess the necessary skills to perform such post-diagnostic skills. Mrs. Wing was an expert.

Lily, after she'd made me a milkshake at the restaurant ice cream counter, loaned me a spoon with a long handle and a tiny scoop at its end. As I was using it to scrape up the last bits of delicious ice cream from the bottom of the empty milkshake glass, Lily casually said, "My mother used a spoon like that to dig out the poop from the bum holes of many constipated elderly men whom she nursed back to health after Doc Stewart confessed there was nothing he could do for them." I doubt that Lily's vivid story dissuaded me from rescuing ice cream dregs from the bottom of my empty milkshake glass. But now that I am older, I can appreciate Lily's wonderful sense of humour and perfect timing for telling a story.

I do not remember the details of my mother's recovery except that Mrs. Wing kept her in a corner of the Wings' living room, protected from any hustle-bustle or noise that disturbed her rest.

Unnecessary visitors were unwelcome, and although I was a daily visitor, while my mother was still very weak from loss of blood, I was allowed only to go to her bedside, say hello, and tell her I hoped she would be well soon. She didn't speak, only nodded a little and tried to smile. I was never allowed near my mother when they washed her, fed her, removed her bedpan, or changed her bedding. Katy Wing and Mrs. Wing were always at hand to remove me and give me something to do before I returned to where my father and older brother were framing the new house.

Mrs. Wing, I'm sure, examined my mother's urine and stool samples daily. And I presume my mother was kept on a liquid diet, probably beef extract like Bovril and maybe chicken soup from the restaurant.

I never knew how Mrs. Wing's own children adapted to my mother's presence as a patient. They had become accustomed to such inconveniences. Katy had installed a bedsheet curtain from wall to wall to give my mother privacy—and the Wing family, as well, some sort of privacy from my mother.

The Wing family of two adults and fourteen children were of mixed Chinese and Flathead Indian extraction. The father,

Wing Chow—his Chinese name—was a Marxist refugee from Mongolia only partly fluent in English, and his wife, a Flathead Indian from the USA, was bilingual in native Flathead and English. Neither she nor her fourteen children achieved fluency in Chinese. My mother had already formed a close friendship with Mrs. Wing, who had come to her rescue before with her naturopathic medicinal skills. My mother suffered from pernicious anemia, and only five of her nine pregnancies were live births, the others all ending in miscarriages.

I was a playmate of one of the wing boys, Georgie. He was my age. And I greatly admired Georgie's older brother John, who was about fifteen years old at the time. He came into the restaurant kitchen that day, patted my shoulder, and told me not to worry, that my mother would be okay. John was like an affectionate big brother to me. He had been coached by his father, he told me many years later when we met in Burnaby, to always look after his younger siblings. He was also given the daunting role of caretaker of the restaurant's kitchen garden, grown every spring and summer on the rented lot between the restaurant and the adjacent Church of England on Main Street. When we met in Burnaby and reminisced about our childhoods in Lillooet, John informed me that the damned garden tending, without pay from his father, was the main reason why he left home at eighteen and never went back to Lillooet.

His older sister Jennie, whom I thought the prettiest woman in Lillooet, was one of the cooks in their father's restaurant. She was the pastry chef. I remember how she would call Georgie and me in from play, sit us down in the back of the kitchen, and give us each a fork and a generous plate of apricot pie. Apricot trees grew in abundance throughout the town, and fresh apricots were a daily part of my diet, but Jenny's apricot pie was absolute perfection!

I must have always been in a sad state of mind whenever I

visited my mother. I was overcome by worry, knowing there was nothing I could do but wait until she recovered her health. I remember Mrs. Wing saying softly to her children, "Mrs. Whitney has to have complete rest and quiet in order to get better."

"Yes, Momma," they quietly answered. "We'll be quiet. We have taken some of our toys into the waiting room in the rooming house reception office." Some of the children may have even taken up residence in some unoccupied rooms in the rooming house next to the restaurant.

I suppose Mrs. Wing had advised them that my mother was very, very, ill and could not stand even a small amount of noise. "We want Mrs. Whitney to get absolute quiet so she can sleep as much as possible and let her body rest and get healthy again."

Mrs. Wing's daughter, Katy, was also fiercely protective of my mother. I recall, when I arrived at the Wing home on one of my persistent but brief daily visits, Mrs. Pizzi and her daughter Cora Hendrickson were sitting in the living room area opposite my mother's curtained-off bed, busily gossiping about who-knows-what. They were interrupted a few minutes later by the arrival of a furious, seething Katy Wing. I can hear Katy to this day, confronting the two women and giving them a subdued but vicious tongue-lashing. "How dare you come here where poor Nina is trying to recover? Have you left your manners at home? Or do you have any manners? Have you no concern for Nina, struggling to get her health back? No, of course you don't. You wouldn't care if she died!" Katy, shaking in anger, pushed them toward the door, and, as they slunk past her, she hissed, "Get out of here, and don't you or any of your friends come back ever!"

My mother stayed in the Wings' hospital living room for a good month before Mrs. Wing told her that she could go home —on the condition that she come back immediately if she felt herself getting the least bit sick again. Mrs. Wing and my mother exchanged hugs, and I led my mother by the hand the long way home on flat ground, avoiding the Dips by going up the lane, turning left across the filled-in part, and heading back down the gentle grade to our house, which my father and brother, in my mother's absence, had finally completed. It was at least habitable. Nothing fancy, but I am sure my mother was happy to be on her feet again, and to be in a house, no matter how humble.

Mrs. Wing tended to many of my family and friends over the years. The only time I was forced to turn elsewhere for care was when I contracted typhoid fever in 1936. By provincial order, typhoid patients were rushed to the Lytton Hospital. There I spent nine months, partly to recover from typhoid and also to ensure that I was not a carrier of the disease, liable to re-infect the Lillooet community's water supply on my return. Typhoid fever was an item of provincial concern and therefore a great emergency. My symptoms, confirmed by Dr. Ellis in the Lytton Hospital, were brought by Dr. Ployart, Lillooet's town physician, to the immediate attention of the Ministry of Health and, while I was in hospital, a provincial health medical team was sent to Lillooet to check Cayoosh Creek for typhoid and find the source of the contamination upstream from where we lived.

A typhoid carrier was found! He was a visitor from Vancouver, and the nephew of Harold McNair, who was, coincidently, the foreman of Lillooet's Public Works Department. MrHarold McNair was good friends with Ma Murray, wife of the Lillooet MLA and owner/editor of the *Bridge River Lillooet News*. The younger McNair had recently arrived in Lillooet to live with his uncle. They rented a house located at the junction of Seton Creek and Cayoosh Creek, two and a half miles upstream from where the Whitney family drew, in buckets, their daily water supply. The McNair outdoor toilet was situated, for their convenience, on two logs suspended a few feet over the junction of the two creeks, far enough so as to deposit feces and urine—shit and piss—directly into Cayoosh Creek. This clever arrangement saved the occupants of the McNair house the trouble of properly digging an organic repository for their toilet deposits. Why should they? It was a common belief in Lillooet at that time that creeks, rivers, and lakes purified themselves.

Can we, who are so public-health conscious today, believe that such blatant ignorance was common?

So Cayoosh Creek was being used as an open sewer, two and a half miles upstream from where we drew our water supply, by an unreported and provincially unregistered typhoid carrier!

It was extremely ironic that, in the aftermath of this terrible infraction of the dictates of the BC Ministry of Health, no mention of it was forthcoming from Ma Murray's local *Bridge River Lillooet News*. It should have been at least reported, for the sake of educating the Lillooet citizenry, that lakes, creeks, streams, and rivers were not self-purifying!

And, as is done in today's newspapers, the name of the typhoid carrier should have been reported in Ma Murray's newspaper. Nor was there any follow-up on the punishment of the carrier, nor of the hospital that failed to purify his system of the typhoid bacterium before releasing him back into public life.

Worse still, nothing was done in Lillooet to quash the rumour that the Whitney family had infected Mrs. Fleming and caused her death from "typhoid fever." Mrs. Fleming lived on the glacial bench, which we called the town flat, one hundred feet above our Cayoosh Creek flat and nowhere near the Whitneys' tarpaper shack on the bank of Cayoosh Creek. There could not possibly have been any social connection between the two families, nor between their water supplies. I think the people of Lillooet believed I had sneaked up and defecated in Mrs. Fleming's *private* water supply before I was sent, semi-conscious, to Lytton Hospital, sick and delirious with typhoid fever.

The real cause of Mrs. Fleming's death was never reported, nor was it explained that it could not have been typhoid, because the Fleming family drank the same water from Town Creek as every other family did. And nobody else in Lillooet had gotten typhoid fever from the Town Creek water supply.

Not one person from the upper crust of Lillooet said or did anything to correct the injustice done to my family's reputation. We were poor, and therefore we were losers to be despised.

So you can understand the great service bestowed on us poor, despicable, disadvantaged people by Mrs. Wing, this gifted indigenous woman of Flathead Indian heritage. Her diagnostic skills were excellent. She immediately diagnosed my mother's problem, as did her daughter Katy when she first told Jessie, "Nina has had a miscarriage." Perhaps Mrs. Wing, as a girl, was taught some basic medical skills, such as elevating a female patient's lower body to stop internal bleeding. She may have been taught how to use herbal cures from her tribal confreres. But my guess is that she was simply a bright person who soaked up knowledge quickly and taught herself how to apply it. It is unfortunate she was not able to write an autobiography. But even if she had possessed the necessary literary skills, she was an extremely busy medical practitioner, as well as the wife of a busy restaurant owner. Then, too, she must have been a very active mother to give birth to fourteen healthy children.

Our family owed a huge debt of gratitude to Katy Wing and her mother for saving our mother's life. When Joanne and I attended a Lillooet high school reunion in 2004, I was asked to speak. During my many reminiscences, I lauded especially the memory of Mrs. Wing, the dear lady who, with her medical skill and knowledge, saved my mother's life (while the tender loving care of her daughters Katy and Jessie nursed my mother along). Many of the Wing family in the audience beamed and nodded their approval as I spoke, and came to me later to express their thanks for praising the memory of their mother.

I am ever thankful to the saintly mother of the Wing family. Bless you, Mrs. Wing!

Gordon visiting his mom, Nina on her 78th birthday.

SIXTEEN
AQUA REGIA

Around 1849, the time of the Fraser River gold rush, prospectors from the USA came north from the depleted Californian placer mines and headed up the Fraser Canyon, looking for more placer gold.

Approximately ten thousand years previously, BC had been covered with thick glaciers that continuously flowed southward, eroding the mountains over which they passed and grinding away the rocky surfaces. These ground-up rocks beneath the heavy moving ice contained a variety of minerals such as magnetite, iron oxide—also known to the miners as "black sand"—gold, silver, iron pyrite or fool's gold, and a number of silicates: mica, quartz, agates, garnets, and so on.

When the earth warmed, the glacial ice melted, leaving behind only mountain glaciers, remnants of their former greatness perched on mountaintops. And in the deep valleys, which had been gouged out by the glaciers, lakes were formed as the glacier ice melted. The ground-up sediments contained therein were deposited, layer after layer, into the bottoms of the newly formed lakes.

Over thousands of years, these lakes were breached at their lower ends by meltwater rivers gushing out from the mountain glaciers like the one feeding our present Fraser River. The Fraser River, in its winding southward path, has not only carved out its own deep and narrow riverbed but also left behind remnants of the original lake deposits in the form of sedimentary benches clinging to the sides of its valley. All of this bench material was eventually covered by layers of decayed, organic plant life, making it a fertile site for present-day farms and orchards.

The benches are very picturesque, perched on the sides of the valley high above the Fraser, which flows its muddy, silt-laden way past Lytton, North Bend, Boston Bar, Hope, Fort Langley, and New Westminster, all the way through the Richmond Delta into the Salish Sea.

The Fraser meltwater, over millennia, cut through the mineral-laden lake deposits, performing a continuous sorting action. Silt, the lightest material left behind, quickly floated downstream toward the sea and was deposited at the Fraser mouth as our present Fraser Delta. The heavier matter was left behind in the Fraser Canyon as sand, rounded stones, gravel, and the heavy minerals described above, forming our familiar sand and gravel bars.

These final remnants of the glaciation process were eagerly sought by the invading hordes of placer miners, who conveniently named the gravel bars after themselves. The bars would hopefully be sources of rich deposits of placer gold!

The bars became geographic markers, their names indicating where various groups had dug up the gravel and flushed them through their sluice boxes to recover the fine placer gold. So we have today China Bar, named after a group of Chinese miners who squatted on that particular sandbar on the basis of "first come, first served." Another example is French Bar, twenty-five miles north of Lillooet and probably named after a Frenchman who was the first to come onto that particular bar. The nearby French Bar Creek is likely also named after him. And a map will divulge other historic names such as Hope Bar, Anderson Bar, and Boston Bar.

My companions and I, in patrolling the bank of the Fraser below Lillooet day after day, observed much amateur placer mining activity right below the town. With minimal instruction and a few dollars to construct a basic sluice box, a man could make perhaps two dollars per day. And in my childhood during the Hungry Thirties, two dollars was a considerable amount of money. One could rent a house on Main Street for nine dollars a month.

Sluice box used by Chinese miners in Lillooet, called a "Long Tom".

A miner selected, by guess or by God, a likely sand and gravel bar on the Fraser River. His equipment included a homemade sluice box made of three planks, eighteen by seventy-two inches, nailed together to make a rectangular trough open at the top and bottom. He fitted the bottom of this long, open-to-the air box with a removable rectangular piece of thick Hudson's Bay blanket, on top of which he laid a same-sized removable piece of iron mesh screen. This combo of wood, wool blanket, and steel screen was supported on a wooden stand made from strong two-by-fours, its top end chest-high and its bottom end knee-high. At the top end of the sluice box, the miner placed a contrivance called a hopper: a box with an iron grill halfway down inside, the grill slots close enough together to keep out big rocks and gravel and let only the finer material through.

The miner, standing on the very edge of the river with a long-handled dipper, ladled water into the hopper, forcing the mixture in the sluice box downward over the screen and woollen blanket. Heavy material sank through the screen onto the blanket. Some of the heaviest matter penetrated into the blanket. The rest of the shovelful of gravel exited the bottom of the box and piled up on the ground as useless tailings, which could be shovelled out of the way.

At the end of the day, the miner removed the wool blanket and the black sand from the sluice

box and washed it carefully in a tub of water to remove any fine mud. Then, using a gold pan, the miner separated the black sand from heavier rich minerals, such as gold and platinum. That was his precious reward for all that sweat and tears.

Eventually some placer miners abandoned the hand-dipper method and instead used a gasoline-operated water pump. Thus, some men began to earn five dollars a day. I remember hearing the *put-put-put* of such single-cylinder pumps, day after day in warm sunny weather, in spring, summer, and autumn, up and down the east and west banks of the Fraser River within earshot of the town.

Often, the Larter twins—Peter and Paul—and I would head down to the Fraser just below town to see if we could spot any new placer miners setting up their sluice boxes. It was easy to access the riverbank below town because of the trails the pioneer settlers had made years before. These led from the town bench to Foster's farm just below, then zigzagged down the face of the Foster bench to the riverbank itself.

In our wanderings, we used to look for the resident horned owl that perched during the day high in a certain cottonwood tree. We knew that barn owls, a smaller species, were welcome tenants in barns because they preyed on mice, and we assumed that the bigger horned owl also preyed on mice. Owls were always welcome for that reason.

But one morning I witnessed

a scene that was a trifle shocking. At five o'clock in the morning, before sunup, as I was heading for my favourite fishing pool at the mouth of Cayoosh Creek, I passed Dan Copeland's front yard, where he had just turned out his chickens to forage. I was surprised suddenly to see, a few scant feet above my head, a big horned owl drop down, pick up one of Dan Copeland's fat Rhode Island hens, and carry her off for his breakfast. Owls can fly silently, and that was why I hadn't heard it approaching behind me—and the chickens hadn't heard it either. But I reasoned that the owl had as much right to a chicken dinner now and then as we humans did.

One Sunday morning, as Peter, Paul, and I were patrolling the riverbank below Mrs. Foster's farm, we were surprised to see two of Mrs. Foster's Chinese farm labourers setting up a sluice box at the edge of the Fraser River. At least I was surprised. But Paul said, "I've seen them a couple o' times in the back of Parks' store, where Fun Park weighs out placer gold for miners and pays them so much an ounce. So they must have been working some other spot on the river before they moved in here."

"Gold, you should know," Peter chimed in, "is worth thirty-five dollars an ounce."

"Holy cow," I said. "Thirty-five an ounce. I've never seen that much money, ever. I wonder how much gold these Chinese guys will make from their weekly sluicing. Maybe it's more than Mrs. Foster pays them."

"Who knows?" said Paul. "But the poor buggers will be lucky if they make even two dollars a week sluicing in this section of the river. It must have been worked over dozens of times."

"Yeah," said Peter, "but gold is where you find it. And who knows how much gold the old Fraser River is carrying every day as it flows by right in front of our eyes?"

"Dream on!" said Peter. "But they'll keep on trying. I've seen them a few times in the back of Parks' store, having their gold weighed. They never seem very happy with the results."

"Well," I said, "it's handy for them in this spot. They can sluice for gold right below where they work."

We stood, peering at the two farm labourers as they shovelled gravel into their sluice box and used their long-handled dippers to pour water onto the gravel and flush it down the sluice box.

Their faces seemed familiar, but I never did learn their names. I had often spotted the two of them outside their cabin below the railroad tracks, whenever I was walking along the PGE right of way on my way home from school. Their bunkhouse was located on the western edge of Mrs. Foster's farm. I used to see the smaller man out in their woodpile, gathering armloads of firewood to take into their cabin. And once I saw him chopping up something that looked like a large dried fillet of white fish on their big chopping block. "Why not use a meat cleaver like the cook does in See Hing Lung's kitchen?" I wondered to myself.

I had asked my pal Clifford Jim about the fish, but all he could tell me was that his father, the proprietor of Jim brothers' general store, ordered his dried fish on a regular basis from a wholesaler in Vancouver's Chinatown.

The two farmhands worked at sluicing on the river every weekend. They probably dreamed of striking it rich, finding a small fortune in gold trapped in the woollen blanket during their daily cleanup. Cleaning up involved carefully removing the fine mesh screen and the woollen blanket from the bottom of the sluice box and gently placing the swollen blanket into a large, shallow gold pan for the purpose of cleaning out the fine-grained material it contained. Then, squatting in the water at the edge of the river, their feet protected by their heavy rubber boots, they dipped the big gold pan into the water until it rested on some stones. Holding the pan steady with their rubber-booted feet, they would squeeze the woollen blanket section by section with their hands until it surrendered into the pan all the day's accumulated fine material. This would be mostly black sand and hopefully some fine grains of gold.

After squeezing out its contents, they replaced the woollen blanket and wire mesh in the bottom of the sluice box. Picking up the gold pan, one of them drained out as much water as possible and scraped what was left of the fine material into a bucket to take home for further panning.

Their hope was to do a final thorough cleaning by filling the pan with tap water and swirling it with its front side tipped downward, washing most of the fine, lighter material out of the gold pan onto the ground.

Who knew when one might get lucky and find a rich pocket of gold-bearing gravel washing through the sluice box, or a small fortune gleaming up at you from the bottom of the pan?

One Sunday, Peter, Paul, and I went down the trail below Mrs. Foster's farm and strolled over to where the two Chinese men were quietly wo

rking. We used to sit on boulders or a log to watch them for a half hour or so. We had nothing better to do.

The men would grin and nod to us as they went through their routine, digging up gravel, shovelling it into the hopper at the upper end of their sluice box, and removing any large stones before pouring water from the river onto the gravel to wash it down over the wire mesh and woollen blanket.

But, unknown to the two miners and to me, Peter and Paul had hatched a scheme to "salt" their sluice box with brass filings. Their father, Jim Larter, was the Lillooet blacksmith and an automobile mechanic. He often had to reline a brass bearing, which involved much filing with a steel file to achieve an exact fit. So Peter was able to scrape off his father's workbench a considerable quantity of brass filings, which he carried this Sunday in a leather drawstring pouch in his denim shirt pocket.

While we watched, Peter secretly transferred brass filings from the pouch into his left hand. When prompted by Paul to come and admire the fine workmanship of the sluice box, Peter came and bent over the box, supposedly to get a closer look at its workmanship, and deftly sprinkled brass filings onto the gravel as it washed by his face.

Of course, the shiny brass filings

immediately sank out of sight through the wire mesh and disappeared into the absorbent woollen blanket. The salting had been completed without either of the miners having an inkling of what had happened.

Peter and his brother grinned smugly as they backed away

from the sluice box. To the two miners, Peter said, "That is a good sluice box. You guys are good at making things."

"I like your long-handled dippers too!" said Paul.

Both miners nodded and smiled their appreciation.

As we were leaving, Peter said to his brother, "I would like to see their faces when they go to Parks' store to have Fun weigh their gold. You know what is going to happen, don't you?"

"I sure do," said Paul, "and I, for one, don't want to be there when it happens!"

"What do you mean?" I asked. "What can happen? Fun will weigh their gold and pay them at the going rate of thirty-five dollars an ounce, won't he?"

"Ha! You don't know what Fun has to do to test if their gold is real or fake," said Peter.

"What do you mean?" I asked. "Fake gold?"

"I'd better explain to Gordie about aqua regia," Paul broke in. "Aqua regia"—meaning "royal water" in Latin—"is a mixture of two acids, sulphuric acid and nitric acid. This mixture won't dissolve gold, but it will dissolve fake gold, such as brass or copper or iron pyrites. And when it does, it gives off a telltale cloud of thick, poisonous, dark smoke."

Peter grinned broadly. "I guess, Gordie, you didn't see me sprinkle brass filings into their sluice box when they weren't looking."

"Salting is illegal," Paul continued. "Those two Chinese miners will think they've struck it rich when they clean up and see all that fake gold shining up at them out of their gold pan."

"So when Fun pours the aqua regia onto their fake gold," said Peter, "it will all go up in smoke, and they'll panic. They'll think that all their gold is gone, and they'll immediately blame Fun."

That is exactly what happened when the two innocent miners took their "gold" into the back of Parks' store and handed it to Fun for his usual assessment. The sight of their gold disappearing in a dark, explosive cloud completely unnerved them. They panicked and yelled their heads off! It took Fun a long, long ten minutes to calm them down.

Fun explained that they had been "salted" by someone putting brass filings into their sluice box. They were stunned, then angry, then utterly furious. It must have dawned on them that we boys were responsible. And they would have included me in their condemnation, even though I was never near their sluice box. But who could blame them?

I heard about the incident later from Tom Manson, who was in Parks' store when it all happened. "You should have heard them screaming and swearing in Chinese!" said Tom, chuckling at the memory of their outburst. Tom couldn't stop grinning as he told me the details.

But I wasn't grinning. I was frightened at the thought of what the two Chinese miners would do to me if I ever ran into them on the street. So we three miscreants banished from our minds any thought of ever visiting that part of the Fraser shore again. I really feared the two miners would catch us, throw us into the river, and laugh at us as we drowned.

We Lillooet children should have been taught by parents to respect our elders. We weren't, and I felt the fear and shame of it every time I avoided my accustomed shortcut home from school along the PGE railroad tracks because it passed by the shack of the two Chinese placer miners.

SEVENTEEN
THE ROOF

Plop, plop, plop. I heard raindrops hitting the patchwork comforter I was lying under. I sat up with a start and leaped out of bed.

I stared angrily up at the bare roof boards above me. I could see the rainwater running along the edge of a length of shiplap in the ceiling, eventually meeting resistance and dripping onto the bed.

The comforter was already damp where the rain was hitting it. And the wetness was spreading. The whole comforter would have to be taken off, hung up, and dried. Goddammit to hell!

I lifted the end of the bed and swung it sideways, dragging it on its casters out of the path of the rainwater dripping from above.

"Goddammit, goddammit, goddammit!" I cursed as I went downstairs to fetch a new lard pail.

Coming back up the wooden steps, I strode over to the leak and put the pail on the floor under it. I looked around in dismay at the other three lard pails scattered around the upstairs bedrooms, busily catching drips from the leaky roof above. I crumpled up a piece of old newspaper lying on the

139

floor and put it into the bottom of the new pail to muffle the sound of rainwater hitting the shiny metal bottom.

Why in hell hadn't my father, Reuben—or Reub, as people called him—had the energy to shingle all of the roof, front and back? This was the third home we had inhabited in Lillooet, and my father had obviously shingled only the front part, the part facing the back alley at the bottom of our yard, so that anyone walking along the roadway and the back of Wing's yard would think that the whole Whitney roof was shingled. But he'd left the bedrooms in the back half of the house unprotected from rain. What kind of goddamn stupidity was that? Shingling a roof was an easy job. I concluded that my father was lazy. No two ways about it.

Two years before, when I was only seven, I had helped my oldest brother, Ernie, shingle Grandpa Reynolds's outhouse down on Cayoosh Creek. You just had to put two nails into the centre of a shingle to fasten it to the tarpaper and the shiplap underneath. Then you nailed the top edge, one nail on each side. I also knew, from watching my father, how to place shingles on a horizontal wooden guide strip, making sure that each new shingle in the second row covered the space between the two shingles in the row underneath.

Ernie told me that shingling a large roof was as easy as shingling a small one. The important part was correctly installing the very first row of shingles, the starter row. That was painstaking, but not too damned hard. All you had to do was bring shingles up the ladder and heave them onto the plank walkway that ran the length of the scaffolding of two-by-fours, selecting suitable shingles and placing them in a row on the starter strip, ready for nailing. The hardest part was to make sure that each new row of shingles was lined up horizontally, an easy enough task if you were careful and used a guide strip. A child could do it! For a man of my father's carpentry talents, shingling the back portion of the roof would have taken only three or four hours. It wasn't a big roof, and he even possessed an automatic shingle nail dispenser.

My nine-year-old mind toyed with the idea of breaking open a bundle of cedar shingles and getting them safely up the ladder and onto the catwalk. That would be the hardest part for me, besides the danger of falling off the roof!

When I came home from school one day, I went around to the back of the house and stared at the neatly stacked bundles of cedar shingles, twenty-four bundles in all. You could smell them even when they had been rained on. Cedar had a nice smell. I used to make arrows for my rubber band arrow gun out of abandoned shingles. The straight cedar grain made for easy carving with my jackknife.

Behind me, I could see the two-by-four scaffolding was still intact. Just to be sure, I tested it by pushing really hard on the two-by-fours supporting the catwalk. They were solid. Then I tested the catwalk itself by reaching up, grabbing the shiplap, and pulling it up and down. It looked solid enough to stand on, so I climbed up the ladder and walked the first few feet of the catwalk. Yeah, it was okay.

Maybe when my oldest brother Ernie came home from Vancouver for a week in September, as he'd promised, I could ask him to finish shingling the roof. The weather would be good. Lillooet people called September "Indian summer."

One Saturday at five o'clock, a week before Ernie was due to arrive on the PGE passenger train from Squamish, my father and I were shopping in Wo Hing's grocery store. One of the things we picked up was a big piece of salt pork. Salt pork had to be cooked in a special way. Fat chunks of it were first parboiled for fifteen minutes in a frying pan full of boiling water. That was the way to remove the salt that was used to preserve it. Then that frying pan was drained of the salty water, and the pork was fried in it just like bacon. The fat would eventually crisp up, but only a little. Depression food!

It started to get dark as we left the store with our few groceries in my backpack.

We turned left off Main Street down Eagan's Alley, walked past Jim Larter's blacksmith shop, and turned right again at Wing's back alley. We were headed for the Dips and the steep trail across Town Creek gully to our gate.

It was now dark enough for the scattered street lights hung on telephone poles to come on, and one had to walk with care to avoid anything dropped on the roadway, including horse manure from Saturday's wagon traffic up and down the back lanes and alleys.

As we turned into Wing's alley, we had to veer around Baptiste Frank's light, horse-drawn wagon. To our immense surprise, as we steered around the wagon, we saw Baptiste squatting on the ground, hunched over, holding his horse's head in his hands, and sobbing.

The animal was on its side, unharnessed and unhitched from the wagon. The sight of a horse lying on the ground was unnatural and scary. The one time I did see a horse lying on its side was at the first-of-July rodeo. A team in the chuckwagon race had collided with the track's lodgepole-pine railing, which had speared the side of the inside horse with a broken pointed section of railing.

The horse had lain on the track with its insides spilling from its pierced stomach. My uncle Alvin, rodeo marshal, was called over. One look told him the horse was done for. He shot it in the head with his starter pistol and put the animal out of its misery.

My father and I stopped and stared at the scene before us. Then my father quickly knelt and put his hand on Baptiste's shoulder. "Baptiste, what's happened to your horse?"

"Reub," Baptiste answered, "I don't know how it happened, but my horse just now got sick and lay down on the ground. I can't get him up."

"Let me have a look at him," my father said and, still

squatting, moved along the horse's body, feeling the backbone, legs, and stomach from head to rear. Then he bent his head and put his ear to the horse's stomach, pressing down hard on it with both hands. The horse let out a sharp groan.

"Baptiste, your horse has got colic, real bad colic, and he's in terrible pain. You heard him groan when I pressed on his stomach. His stomach and intestines must be full of gas. See how his side, his stomach wall, is bloated?"

"Jeez, Reub, what can I do? I never seen anything like this before. Is my horse gonna die? I hate to see him suffer like his. Will he have to be put down?" Baptiste shuddered, his whole upper body in spasm.

"Look, Baptiste," my father said, "I've seen horses with colic before, and we can save him if we're not too late. But you have to run to See Hing Lung's store, get a gallon of linseed oil, and bring it to me as quick as you can. If See Hing Lung doesn't have it, then go to Jim brothers' store. And if Jim brothers' doesn't have it, go to Parks' store. And hurry!"

Baptiste ran off as if he'd been shot from the barrel of a cannon.

Meanwhile, my father held the horse's head in his hands, stroked it, and said soothingly, "Don't you worry, now. You're gonna be all right as soon as I can get some linseed oil inside you. Baptiste must have been feeding you mouldy hay, and now your insides are full of gas, but I'm gonna get the gas out of your stomach and intestines. You're gonna be okay, I promise you." He was still stroking the horse's ears and forehead when Baptiste returned, clutching a gallon jug full of the linseed oil.

"Gordon," my father said calmly to me, "take the jug from Baptiste and uncork it. Be careful not to spill any. Put it on the ground near me so I can reach it when I need it." Then he turned to Baptiste. "Baptiste, you are going to gently lift up the horse's head and put your knee under his neck so I can force open his jaws. Then, with your two hands, you're going to have to hold his jaws gently apart while I slowly pour the linseed oil into him. You understand?"

Baptiste nodded, keeping his eyes fixed intently on Reuben's face. Then my father carefully lifted the jug and started to pour a steady, slow *drip, drip, drip* of oil into the horse's mouth, pausing between drips to let the horse swallow without choking. I could see that my father had done this many times before. He had to have done, because everything went so smoothly.

And then I realized that ever since my father had first touched the stricken horse, his whole body, his face, his hands, his clothing, everything he touched—even the horse's body as he stroked it—had begun to glow with a faint golden light. I looked around. Nothing else had changed colour!

I closed my eyes shut tight. When I slowly opened them, the colour was still there. My father was still bathed in glowing gold: his hands, face, clothing, the linseed oil jug, the oil as it flowed into the horse's mouth, and the horse's body too, from head to tail. Everything my father touched was glowing.

I was frightened. What was happening? I was so overcome that I had to turn my head away and sob softly into my shirt sleeve.

"Okay," my father whispered. "Baptiste, you can gently rub your horse's stomach, legs, and back. I'll hold his head, talk to him, and rub his face, neck, and ears. He's gonna be all right now. In a few minutes, he should start farting, and once that happens, keep rubbing. We can eventually try to get him onto his feet. Keep rubbing his body, especially his stomach, from front to back, to help him pass all the gas out of his guts."

Baptiste's horse began to fart and continued to do so for several long minutes. Gently, Baptiste and my father coaxed the horse to roll over just enough to assume a kneeling position, and then they finally coaxed him to stand up on his shaking feet, emitting one last, long, loud, acrid fart that stung my nostrils.

My father resumed talking to the horse, which seemed to reply by nodding its head and emitting a low-pitched snuffle as if to say, "Thanks for saving my life." There were tears in my eyes as I gazed at my father with deep satisfaction, a sensation I had never felt before. Baptiste also had tears of gratitude in his eyes as he grasped Reuben's hands in his own.

"Reub," Baptiste said, "how can I thank you for savin' my horse? I really thought he was gonna die. I wanna give you somethin', but all I have are some carrots." He went to his wagon and lifted out a gunny sack full of carrots, which he put on the ground in front of my father and opened to show its contents. Baptiste had dug up the carrots that day from his garden plot on the Cayoosh Creek Indian Reserve.

"You don't have to give me anything, Baptiste," said Reuben. "I'm glad I could be here in time to help you save your horse. Look at him now. He'll be strong enough in an hour or so to pull your wagon home. And once you get to Station Hill, it's downhill all the way to your place on the reserve. All you have to do now is give him some fresh drinking water. You can fill your hat with water from Jim Larter's garden tap. Don't feed your horse anything until morning. He needs to give his stomach a good rest. Tomorrow, make sure he gets good fresh hay."

"Reub," Baptiste insisted, "you gotta take this sack of carrots. I'm not gonna let you go until you say you'll take 'em. I can carry 'em to your front porch right now. Maybe your boy can show me the way."

"Okay," said my father. He turned to me. "Gordon, go with Baptiste and show him the way. I want to stay with the horse until Baptiste gets back."

After Baptiste and I reached the front porch, and he had put the sack of carrots carefully next to the front door, he turned to me and said, "Your father, Reuben, he's a great man. You're a lucky boy to have him for a father. You just now seen what he done. I'll never forget him, never."

I was really impressed by my father's performance. But why did he try to refuse the gift from Baptiste? After all, he had saved Baptiste's horse from dying of colic, and we could really use the carrots. Food was never abundant in the Whitney household.

When my father came home, I realized that the golden glow was gone from his body. I could not understand why the glow had appeared in the first place, or why, an hour later, it disappeared.

I admit I was a superstitious person. Maybe, just maybe, an angel had something to do with the eerie, golden glow. I think I did believe in angels as my grandmother did, even though my Sunday school teacher, Paul Marlatt, only mentioned angels at those times in the New Testament when Jesus created miracles before he was crucified. But Mr. Marlatt said there was good in every one of God's children. You just had to look for it, and it was harder to find in some people than in others.

I concluded that my father was one of the harder ones. But maybe the miracle of saving Baptiste's horse was a real sign from heaven that a change had taken place in my father's soul, in his mind, in his sense of responsibility to his family — extending even to the leaky roof. I went to sleep that night very relieved and happy. I believed my father had been changed by a miracle.

But as the week passed, and no effort was forthcoming from my father concerning the un-shingled half of the roof, even after it rained three days later, doubt began to creep back into my mind. And when Ernie arrived from Vancouver, and he and Allan completed the shingling of the roof in one day, I became convinced that my father worked only when he could get recognition and praise from strangers.

Perhaps my father had been born lazy, or maybe something bad had happened to him when he was growing up. Maybe his father had done something to him to make him think that family wasn't important.

I recalled the time my father had rewired the motor of Joe Pizzi's old Ford truck and refused to be paid for it. And there was the time he helped Blackie Blackburn put a new front door on his house on Main Street. Blackie couldn't figure out how to hang the door plumb in its frame so that it opened and closed properly, and Reuben did it perfectly in two hours. Blackie had offered Reuben two dollars, a lot of money in those times, but my father had accepted only a pair of inexpensive electrician's pliers instead.

Yes, I mused, recognition from strangers was what motivated my father. Family didn't count!

I made up my mind then and there that I was not going to grow up to be like my father. I was going to get an education, go to university, become a teacher, own a piece of land, and build a house on it: a beautiful house with a beautiful garden.

And if ever I got married and had children, their house, their home, would *never, ever have a leaky roof!*

Whitney family home in Burnaby, designed and built by Gordon.

147

Gordon and his garden, 1990.

EIGHTEEN
FRENCHY THE PLACER MINER

Cayoosh Creek, the sound of its clear green water rushing to join the Fraser River a mile below the wooden trussed bridge on the road south from Lillooet, will always remain etched vividly in my memory. I recall with pleasure the many happy hours I spent as a boy, crouching my way furtively along its rocky banks and finding a pool deep enough to give cover to any unwary rainbow trout.

Many a morning in summer found me, at five o'clock, getting out of bed, dressing hurriedly, eating a sandwich breakfast I had prepared the night before, and packing two sandwiches and an apple into my fishing creel, which I'd made out of an empty cardboard beer carton and some gunny-sacking for an inner liner and outer cover. To this I lashed three-quarter-inch hemp rope tightly to the holes I had made in the end of the creel. This was the carrying strap.

With my shirt pockets stuffed with fly hooks and nylon leader, and a homemade fishing pole in my hand, I would sneak quietly out the back door of our rented house so as not to wake the rest of my family. I would walk down Main Street in my fishing clothes, patched denim jeans and old running shoes, and head for Cayoosh Creek a mile below the town.

At the southern end of Main Street, I would cross the PGE railroad tracks and cut straight south across a sagebrush flat to the cliff edge, where I stood momentarily, looking down on the Cayoosh Creek flats below.

A steep zigzag path carved into the cliff allowed me to run from sturdy pine to sturdy pine, the pylons of the footpath, arriving breathless onto the flat below. There, at the bottom, I could step out onto the sand and gravel expanse of the Cayoosh Creek flat. Saskatoon and chokecherry bushes studded the flat while the ubiquitous fireweed plants showed off their long, lilac blooms of summer. A final walk of a hundred yards took me to the creek bank, its edge a few feet above the green water rushing by on its last dash to the Fraser River. I could see the river by turning my eyes eastward and peering through the wooden trusses of the Station Hill automobile bridge.

Once I was down at the water's edge, I could sit quietly on a boulder or driftwood log and find myself reborn in a green world. With the creek in front of me and the alder and cottonwood trees behind me, I was separated from the human sounds that echoed in the town above.

If I sat still for a few minutes, I could usually spot a duck or two resting on the surface of a large upstream pool or, on the opposite side of the creek, a small adult dipper bird diving into an eddy formed by a log or a rock. It would disappear beneath the surface, searching for aquatic insects invisible to my eye in the turbulence of the creek water. But the creek proved a suitable hunting ground for a dipper bird's *carte du jour* of protein-rich food for itself and its nestlings.

Cayoosh Creek was my second home. I liked being there. I liked thinking about it. I used to wonder why they called it a creek. It was at least one hundred yards wide on the flat where my grandparents lived, and often ten feet deep. It did narrow three miles upstream, where it plunged over a 150-foot waterfall that we called the Falls. And above the Falls, the creek narrowed in a few places to a rapidly flowing two hundred feet in width. One could easily throw a rock across it.

As a boy, I never did follow the creek more than a mile or two above the Falls, a small portion of its twenty-five-mile course up to its source, Duffy Lake. Nowadays, any tourist can drive its full upper length, and as a result, the once-inaccessible creek, full of large rainbow trout, has been fished out.

When I was a boy, if you went upstream from the wooden bridge at the foot of Station Hill, there was no way to cross from the north side to the south side of the creek until you reached George Minchin's place, a lonely cabin two miles upstream. It was perched on a small bench of land fifty feet above the high-water mark across the creek.

At that point in the creek, If you were agile and brave enough, you could—like an aerialist, a tightrope walker, a circus performer—cross the creek from the north side to the south side by walking across the dangerous "twin-steel telephone wire bridge" suspended in air six feet above the water.

Some clever placer miners had, several years previously, found—or "liberated"—their own bridge-building material: several hundred feet of steel telephone wire about an eighth of an inch in diameter. With this, they were able to construct a tightrope "high-wire" bridge across the creek. They did this by tethering one end of the wire to the trunk of a huge fir tree on the north side of the creek, carrying the loose end of the wire bulk across the creek when the water level permitted, and tethering it to a similar tree trunk on the south side. The wire was manually stretched as taut as possible, about six feet above the flowing creek.

This process was duplicated from south side to north side to produce a second wire, parallel to the first but three feet higher and staggered one foot downstream, so that when you were crossing, you would stand leaning slightly forward, with two feet on the lower wire and two hands grasping the upper wire to avoid falling backward and being drowned in the water rushing underneath.

In order to mount or dismount the wire on each side of the creek, they built stairs from purloined planks and firmly lashed them to the original tree trunk with heavy, coated wire. The user could climb the stairs, stand upon the bottom wire, clutch the upper wire, and begin a simple synchronized shuffling of feet and hands sideways, inching cautiously toward the other side. Then he could climb down another set of stairs and stand once more on solid ground. He would have found it advisable to avoid looking down at the raging creek water beneath him.

What a remarkable structure, and what a remarkable feat of balance, shuffling 150 feet over fast-flowing water!

The danger to intrepid fisherman did not end there, however. Once you left the wires and got onto the path that led to the foot of the Falls, you could, with difficulty and courage, climb 150 feet up the Falls alongside a cascade of water roaring, foaming, and frothing its way from the narrow upper canyon down to the placid creek below.

Once you were at the top of the Falls, a path led one hundred feet further upstream to a dangerous homemade log bridge that allowed you to cross to the north side of the creek and get safe, easy access to a series of rich trout fishing pools upstream. The log bridge had been built by prospectors or fur trappers years before. They had felled a fir tree on the north side of the creek, close enough to the edge to actually span the creek as it fell onto the south side. They trimmed the excess branches and strung one taut strand of telephone wire across the gap to serve as a handhold as the user cautiously placed his feet on the log and inched his way across.

I was never brave enough to try the dual-wire crossing, and I don't think any of my fishing companions ever felt the urge to demonstrate the necessary bravado. The promise of an abundance of good-sized rainbow trout, awaiting them in Fisherman's Paradise, fell on deaf ears. We always fished on just one side, either the south or north side of the creek, which involved a long, tiring trek from either end of the Station Hill Bridge three miles downstream.

But some more courageous boys did use the high-wire bridge, and, after precariously shuffling across on the wires from the north side, proceeded further upstream on the south side to face the second, more dangerous hazard of the log bridge. I preferred fishing my way up from the south end of the Station Hill Bridge, stopping short of the base of the Falls. I was chicken. And I easily dissuaded the less courageous boys in my company from trying to climb the Falls. The horrible sound and frightening appearance of the Falls, even from our safe distance, was evidence of the obvious danger.

They accepted my advice. They couldn't bring themselves to even think about looking for the wet, slippery, well-worn path that led up past the frothing cataract to the fish-rich canyon above.

But one day, my fishing buddy, Georgie Wing, taunted me, calling me a coward, and convinced me that I had to climb the Falls as a sort of rite of passage. He tried to ease my fears by saying, "Hey, Gordy, let's go up to George Minchin's cabin. It's right above us. We can climb the Falls after we bum something to eat. George Minchin makes good pancakes and always has some left over from his breakfast." So we climbed the short cut-off path to George Minchin's cabin and knocked on his door. He was not happy to see us, but he invited us in. It was *noblesse oblige* of a sort.

The pancakes were okay, but instead of syrup to top them, he offered us sour chokecherry jam. We hated to be impolite and refuse, so we accepted his offer. I guess he couldn't afford sugar. The jam was really bitter. I can still remember how it puckered my lips. But we were too hungry to mind, and I carefully rolled up my jam-laden pancake and put one end in my mouth, forcing a smile after each bite. Looking back, I suppose we were lucky to be offered pure, nutritious, natural jam with no harmful additives.

I made the climb, very frightened the entire time. My sour meal of pancakes now seemed poor payment for facing the danger ahead. If I strayed too close to the edge of the path and lost my footing on a slippery rock surface, I could surely stumble and meet sudden death by bashing, unconscious, into the rock wall and drowning. I remember how the steep path was wet and slippery from the spray of foaming water that crashed a few feet from my face. And the deafening noise of the waterfall convinced me that I was risking my life for nothing more than the pleasure of catching an oversized rainbow trout.

When I got to the top the Falls and saw the homemade log bridge to the north side of the creek, the prospect of death seemed even more certain. One misstep, one failed handhold, would result in instantaneous, violent death in the Falls, twenty-five feet away from where I was standing.

I only ever made the climb twice: first with my old pal Georgie, and the second time with Bobby Hurley, whose father was an avid fly fisherman like myself.

On my way home after my second ascent, I met Tom Manson coming down Station Hill.

"Hey, Gordy," Tom said as we sat on the shady side of the road beside the water tank. "Shorty Laidlaw said that you and your pals have started fishing above the Falls."

"Yeah," I replied. "We were after the big rainbow trout everyone brags about."

"And," said Tom, "did you have any luck?"

"We sure did. Bobby Hurley and I each caught ten fat twelve-inch trout in one hour. That was more than enough for one day, so we left the creek and hiked home."

"Did you climb the Falls at George Minchin's cabin, or did you go up the big hill from Seton Lake?"

"We climbed the Falls at George Minchin's cabin and came

down by Seton Lake," I replied. "Bobby wanted to take the shorter way down the Falls on the way back, but I refused. It's too dangerous, and that log bridge at the top of the Falls is too scary for me. Who built the path up beside the Falls, and who built the bridge at the top, the one with the telephone wire for a handrail? Was it George Minchin, looking for gold up Cayoosh Canyon?"

"Well," said Tom, "it could have been George Minchin. There was a lot of prospecting going on in the upper Cayoosh Canyon twenty years ago. You heard about the Golden Cache mine, didn't you? It was a failure, but that didn't stop the dreamers. They figured that the glacier, back ten thousand years or so, could have calved off a lot of gold-bearing quartz and ground it into the creek, where it was waiting to be discovered at the bottom of a sluice box."

"Did anyone find any gold?" I asked.

"Not yet, but that doesn't stop them from looking," Tom said. "Frenchy Bleuis is up there now, working on a wing dam. He's from Quebec. He's got the gold fever pretty bad. But let him have his fun. He is as strong as an ox and as stubborn as a mule. I wish him luck. But I hear the booze has got him. I hope he knows how dangerous the creek can be. Christ, if you fall in? Fast, ice-cold water and alcohol don't mix. And Gordy, you know about the Falls."

I nodded, eyes wide and struck dumb.

"If that damned fool Frenchy gets drunk and falls into the creek, he'll drown. A man can drown in six inches of water if he's knocked unconscious and falls face down. Even if Frenchy didn't drown, he'd be carried downstream, and in a flash he'd be over the Falls and down into the Fraser River at the Cayoosh mouth. It'd be goodbye, Frenchy. Maybe they'd fish his body out at Hope or even Vancouver."

Tom's long soliloquy really shook me up. I imagined myself caught in the current and swept over the Falls. Tom saw my fear, and the drops of sweat on my forehead. He put his hand on my shoulder. "I'm sorry if I scared you, Gordy, but I'd rather have you scared about the Falls than have you reported drowned in them. You should warn all your pals. There have been several deaths on the creek. Three years ago, Boyce Dickey and Frank Vinal drowned while working on a placer gold claim in Cayoosh. No." He stopped himself. "I'm wrong. Those two were drowned in the Fraser River, trying to tow a load of lumber behind their rowboat. They had a placer claim on the east side of the river they thought would really pan out. They found lots of colours when they tested it the week before."

"Artie Phair," Tom continued, "was watching them from his back porch through his binoculars. Artie said they made it about halfway across when the lumber shifted, came untied, got caught in the current, and nosedived. The tow rope immediately pulled the rear of the rowboat under the water. Artie said they could have saved themselves if they had cut the tow rope, but, hell, there was no time to cut a tow rope. The boat was pulled under, and Boyce and Frank were thrown out of the boat and into the water, then instantly swept out of sight downstream. You don't last long in the ice-cold Fraser River," said Tom frankly. "They found their bodies on a sandbar at Hope three days later."

I got up quickly and leaned against the water tank. Sweat was pouring from my forehead. I was close to tears, I was so terribly frightened. Tom made me sit down. He dipped the communal drinking can in the cold water of the tank and made me sip some water slowly, slowly, slowly.

We sat there for a good ten minutes before Tom leaned back and slapped his thighs. Then he bent over and looked me directly in the eyes. "Are you okay?" His expression was quizzical. I could not figure out if he was making fun of me, or if he was worried about me.

I heaved a deep sigh and murmured weakly, "Yes, I'm

okay. But Jesus, I'm sure afraid of those Cayoosh Creek Falls after hearing about Boyce Dickey and Frank Vinal."

"Well," Tom said, "that's life. Death is always waiting for careless people to make one small mistake. So you be careful when you're around water — don't make even one small mistake."

I promised Tom that I would be careful and heaved another deep sigh as I got up and walked up Station Hill toward home. After that, I resolved to fish the south side of Cayoosh Creek, working my way up only as far as the base of the Falls. I was content to remain a live chicken instead of a gone goose!

The next week passed okay. School always captured my full attention. I forgot all about the stories Tom Manson had told, and I quietly promised myself that my expeditions climbing the Falls were over and done with. I felt at peace with my Lillooet world.

I had nothing personal planned for the coming weekend, and no plans to go fishing. So I was relieved when my mother received a message from her sister Ruby that we were all invited to Grandmother's chicken ranch on Cayoosh Creek for lunch on Sunday.

I went early so that I could help Grandmother make her homemade noodles. She mixed the dough with lots of butter, eggs, and flour in her huge cream-coloured mixing bowl, poured the mixture onto the floured tabletop, and rolled it to the desired thinness with a large wooden rolling pin. Then she cut it into rectangles that I, with my freshly washed hands, helped to roll into tubes and slice into half-inch strips. I was allowed to use the large butcher knife. Then my brother Ernie tied cotton store twine across the kitchen from wall to wall and, while I held the platter, deftly strung up line after line of noodles to dry in the warm kitchen air.

Suddenly, Aunt Ruby came panting into the kitchen, shouting, "Close all the windows and doors. There's something

rotting in the creek. Can't you smell it? Hurry, or it will stink up
the noodles. It's a terrible rotten smell. Maybe a deer or a horse or
a cow has been drowned. It seems to be coming from the island."

"Ernie," Grandmother said, "you'd better go check on it.
Just get close enough to see what it is. Don't go near it!"

In twenty minutes, Ernie was back. He opened the kitchen
door a crack and shouted in. "It's Frenchy Bleuis. He's been
drowned, and his body is floating on the edge of the big pool at
the south end of the island. I didn't recognize him because his
body is bloated like a balloon. I couldn't see his face, but I
recognized his clothing, and I recognized the big bowie knife
he carried in a scabbard on his belt. It's Frenchy, all right, and
God, does he stink!"

Grandmother said, "Run across the bridge and ask Mrs.
Blackburn to call the police. And tell Constable MacLaughlin
to get here fast because the whole Cayoosh flat stinks of death.
We'll all be getting sick if we have to breathe the poisonous air
much longer." She looked out the window at the washing she
had hung on the clothesline that morning. "I should have
gotten Ernie to bring it in right after breakfast. Now it'll stink
to hell, and I'll have to do the damned washing all over again."

The BC police arrived after a half hour, with a hearse and a
big canvas sack into which they managed to pour Frenchy's
swollen corpse.

On the way back up to town, under the constable's order,
they stopped immediately at the cemetery, where Shorty
Laidlaw, the town gravedigger, had furiously dug a grave.
Shorty was wearing his rubberized raincoat, a toque on his
head, and a large scarf across his face. He climbed out of the
hole and stood back as Frenchy Bleuis's body, still in its canvas
sack, was dumped unceremoniously into the freshly dug hole.
Shorty filled in the grave in record time. Then, leaning on his
shovel, he murmured through his scarf, "What a waste of a
human life." Constable MacLaughlin patted Shorty's shoulder
in sympathy, which caused Shorty to gag. "Christ," he groaned.

"I'm gonna throw up, I'm gonna throw up. Stand back, everybody!" *Harrrrruuuupppp!*

And Shorty, my hobo friend from BC via London, England, vomited his breakfast onto the ground near the final resting place of Frenchy Bleuis from Quebec.

Shorty gathered up his pick, crowbar, and shovel, spread a quick shovelful of dirt on his expensive, regurgitated See Hing Lung's café breakfast, and joined the rest of the gathering as they nodded sympathetically toward Frenchy's grave. They then turned away, ushered by Constable MacLaughlin, to make a sombre exit through the cemetery gate.

All that was needed was someone to softly play "O Canada" on a harmonica.

Gordon fishing in Cayoosh Creek.

Placer mining.

Campfire fish - fry.

Donnie and Robbie, Gordon's sons, with their catch
of the day.

NINETEEN
SETON LAKE

I have often wondered about the origin of the name Seton. I'd guessed that it derived from an indigenous name, but in fact, the lake was named by the fur trader and civil servant Alexander Caulfield Anderson in honour of his drowned cousin, Lieutenant Colonel Alexander Seton. Seton Lake stretches twelve scenic miles along the PGE right of way from its lower eastern end near Lillooet to its upper western end, where it is separated from its twin, Anderson Lake, by a "geologically recent" landslide. This became the site of the Indian village *Sha'lal'th*, later changed to Portage.

Today, the town goes by both Portage and Shalalth, probably due to the presence of several newer commercial buildings. I think this modernization occurred during the aftermath of the gold rush in 1849.

In earlier times, canoeists heading east to Lillooet would have had to land their canoes at Shalalth, disembark, unload their canoes, tote everything overland on foot or by horse, and refloat them again in Seton Lake.

The name Portage is, of course, French. The verb *porter* means "to carry," and the noun *portage* means "the place for, or the act of, carrying." (Try to remember all this because it will be on the test on Monday.)

When I was ten, I had the opportunity to camp overnight with a group of boys as a guest of my elder brother Allan's Boy Scout troop. That was a special treat for me because I had never been on the lake after dark. You could lean back against a tree trunk, crawl into your sleeping bag, and look up at the Milky Way, trying to identify various constellations and stars, coached by one of the older scouts who knew much about astronomy.

I was fascinated by the different personality of the lake after night fell. The night air was so cool and fresh. I even had the chance to see lightning bugs in flight. I had heard about them before, but no one knew how they were able to glow in the night as they searched for mates.

And it was quiet except for the noise of an occasional late-night party at the wharf, one hundred yards down the beach from where we were camped. That was the first time I heard a ukulele being strummed to accompany a woman singing a Hawaiian love song. She had a lovely soprano voice, and I learned later in life that she had taken voice lessons. I have been strumming my ukulele over the years for my own amusement, and when I play the chords for that song, my mind is carried back all those years to that evening on Seton Lake.

I was surprised when I woke on the first morning at five o'clock, crept out of my bed, and looked at the lake below where we were camped. A full moon was still shining on the water from behind the hill, where Harry Carey's big house overlooked the upper reaches of Seton Lake. One could see almost as far as Shalalth, or so I was told. I think you would need a telescope to see that far.

To my surprise and delight, there was not a single ripple on the water. The lake was like a mirror in the moonlight, with no sound of water lapping on the shore as it did in Yeats' poem about Lake Innisfree, with its "low sounds down by the shore."

Every other time I had been at the lake, there were waves on its surface, especially at noon. At that time, the waves were topped with whitecaps. The wind off the lake blew shoreward very briskly, and we were told to stay out of the water because it was too rough for swimming and could be very dangerous if you became too tired to make it back to the wharf and safety. Even a rowboat couldn't rescue you in such rough water.

I went back into my bed and slept until we were wakened to get dressed for a hearty breakfast of pancakes, syrup, and bacon and eggs. We were even given coffee to drink with sugar and condensed milk. I felt quite grown-up.

Seton Lake in the 1920s, after the construction of the Pacific Great Eastern railroad along its northern shore, became a popular tourist site. On a flat piece of land on the north side of the lake, the Craig family from Vancouver built Craig Lodge, right alongside the PGE railroad tracks.

The lobby at the rear of Craig Lodge opened out onto the platform of the train station, which had been built there, three and a half miles west of the larger PGE station in Lillooet, in order to accommodate the hundreds of tourists who flocked from humid Vancouver in summertime to beautiful Craig Lodge on Seton Lake.

The south side of Craig Lodge fronted on the sky-blue waters of Seton Lake and squatted dramatically beneath towering Mission Mountain at its back. A hundred yards to the south, along the curve of the lakeshore, Seton Lake drained into Seton Creek, whose gently flowing shallow waters offered a spot for fly fishermen to try their luck.

A short walk from the front of the lodge placed you on its wharf. There you walked on a spacious, smooth, planked wharf replete with a painted canvas diving board and laddered diving tower that provided excitement and vigorous exercise for guests who wished to show off their diving and swimming skills. A small fleet of rowboats and sailboats, berthed on the landward side of the wharf, provided would-be sailors with a healthy outlet for their freshwater nautical desires. The combination of hot summer air and cool, refreshing, clear lake water must have been absolutely delightful to the paying guests.

We, the local citizenry, were forbidden entry onto Craig Lodge grounds and access to the wharf by adequate signage that warned, *Private Property, Lodge Guests Only*. We, the local lake visitors from town, had our own public wharf on Seton Lake, which I enjoyed regularly as an adolescent during the hot summers.

By this time I was a preteen, and my family had moved from town to a tarpaper shack down on the Cayoosh Creek flats. My dad had built that shack on land that was unoccupied. My parents had tried to move us to the Lower Mainland in the summer of 1935, but when my dad could not find work there, we returned to Lillooet with nowhere to live. My dad built that shack, and technically we were squatters, but we lived there for two years—until we left Lillooet for good in 1939.

Every Saturday morning, I rose early on the flats to fish in Cayoosh Creek. I would start from the car bridge and continue fishing up Seton Creek until I ended up at Seton Lake, a distance of about three miles. I always caught trout on this early morning caper, and at the lake I took them out of my homemade creel and parked them in a small handmade pool on the lakeshore. I stored my fishing pole, creel, and knapsack in a safe storage place on the wharf and joined up with my friends, who had been driven in by their parents around ten o'clock for a morning of swimming and sunbathing. I always had my swimming trunks in my backpack, and it took only a minute or two to duck into the bushes to change. I kept my shirt on while I was out of the water because I burned quite easily.

My backpack was safe on the wharf, and my trout were safely cooling in their little storage pool in the shade on the lakeshore. I had no trouble giving them away, usually to May Jim, in return for a ride back at four o'clock when her brother came to pick her up in her dad's delivery truck. He would drop me off at the Cayoosh Creek Bridge, from where I could see our tarpaper shack simultaneously cooking in the afternoon sun and being cooled by the constant breeze off Cayoosh Creek.

May Jim was always overjoyed at the gift of two or three large rainbow trout. And I was happy to get rid of them because I had trout for dinner often during the week. I loved fishing, and I was good at it. May and I enjoyed a nice, close preteen friendship.

From our wharf, where we warmed up after a dip or two in the cool water, we could look across the lake and watch the Craig Lodge guests diving off the low and high diving boards. We were never tempted to invade the privacy of the posh lodge guests on the wharf because we would have had to swim one hundred yards, a considerable challenge for all except a few of us.

Some folks were great divers. The best was Bertie Craig, son of the lodge owner. His specialty off the high board was the swan dive. Bertie was also a powerful swimmer and often swam the one hundred yards to our wharf to chat with us teenage boys. He was still a bachelor, but he eventually married beautiful Laura Santini, daughter of the owner of Santini's Ice Cream Parlour, and they had a son they named David Arthur, after Bertie's father.

One day, when Bertie climbed up our ladder onto the deck of our plain wharf, he was inundated with praise for his diving skills, especially the swan dive. I remember him saying, "Maybe someday some of you boys can swim over to our wharf, and I can give you some basic training in diving. Maybe some of you will learn to do the swan dive."

George Hurley, a polite, well-mannered preteen, said, "Thanks Mr. Craig, but one hundred yards is too long a swim for most of us. I, personally, would be immediately swept downstream and drowned."

"Well," replied Bertie, "why don't we make you a diving board right here on your own wharf?" He turned to Ernie Marshall, owner of Marshall's Seton Lake ferry service. "Ernie, don't you have a ten-foot, or even an eight-foot plank we could use for a diving board?"

"Sure," Ernie replied. "Look above you, up on the roof of my tool shed. There's a ten-footer right there, and these two boys beside me can easily pull it down."

Soon the plank lay on the deck, and Bertie looked it over carefully. "Yes, that will make a fine diving board."

Ernie Marshall knew exactly what Bertie had in mind, so he drove his car onto the wharf. Four strong boys placed and held the plank in position in the centre, so three feet rested on the wharf and seven feet projected out over the lake. Then Ernie Marshall carefully drove his car forward until its left front wheel rested firmly on the wharf end of the plank. He shut off the motor and put on the emergency brake. Bertie walked out to the end of the plank over the lake, jumped up and down a few times, and we all watched in awe as Ernie Marshall's car bounced slightly up and down in time with Bertie's gymnastics.

Bertie rejoined the crowd of boys and one girl and said, "Perfect! Now we can take turns diving off the end of the plank. But be careful to only walk slowly to the end of the plank—no running allowed. When you are ready to dive, just put your arms horizontally in front of your face, bend your knees, give one bounce down on the board, and, on the upswing, let the board throw you forward into the air, keeping your arms straight in front of your face. At the last moment, looking down before you hit the water, bring your hands together to protect your face as you hit the lake. As soon as all your body is under the water, just tilt your hands upward and, presto, you will rise up to the surface."

Bertie, to demonstrate, walked carefully out on the plank and stopped with his feet just sticking out over the edge. "I'll go first," he said, "and you can watch while I talk myself through the dive. Watch me and listen to what I am saying to myself. You all saw how careful I was as I *walked* out on the plank. I didn't run!"

Bertie made a perfect dive, surfaced, came up the ladder, and dried his face as someone handed him a dry towel. We took several turns as Bertie continued his verbal coaching.

The last one to dive was a girl. When she was finished, Bertie asked her name.

"Neve Pizzi."

"Ah," said Bertie. "Joe Pizzi's daughter. How old are you, Neve?"

"Sixteen," she replied.

"Well," said Bertie, "you dived perfectly each time. Maybe someday you will want to take part in diving competitions in Kamloops. If you wish, I can teach you some technique—that is, if your mother and father will give consent."

Neve beamed at Bertie. "Thank you so much, Mr. Craig. I will ask them right away!"

Bertie nodded and grinned. "Give your parents my regards. But first," he continued, "let's see how good a swimmer you are. I want you to swim beside me over to the lodge wharf and back. We'll take it easy."

So they swam over and back. Neve had no trouble keeping up with Bertie.

Bertie turned to us and said, "I'll see you all tomorrow at two after the lake has calmed down, and we can all do more diving, provided that Mr. Marshall hasn't moved his car off the end of the plank. And remember: no swimming, and no diving, until the lake has calmed down."

Ernie Marshall smiled and nodded his agreement. "We are not allowed to park our cars overnight on the wharf. But I can always drive back onto the wharf, and the boys and I will fix up the diving board the same as we did just now."

They all shouted their goodbyes as Bertie made a final fancy dive off the end of the new plank diving board and swam swiftly across to the Craig Lodge wharf. He climbed out of the lake and gave a final backhand wave to the admiring group of young, would-be divers.

One Saturday afternoon, a large group of us bystanders were gawking at the seaplane that was tied to the south side of the wharf as Blackie Blackburn worked on its engine. The seaplane's engine had stalled just as its pilot had begun taxiing toward the wharf to let off his passenger, a mining engineer on a monthly visit to the Bralorne mine. It was lucky the plane hadn't stalled in flight. Otherwise the result would have been a nasty accident. After several hours' work, the pilot checked the engine as Blackie cocked an intelligent ear to the sound it was making. "Smooth as a peach," he shouted as the pilot revved the motor up and down.

The pilot proceeded to reload his belongings into the rear of the plane. Then he watched carefully from where he stood on a pontoon as Ernie Marshall tugged the plane free of the wharf with his rowboat. The pilot climbed back into his seat and waved to Ernie to keep towing the plane toward the centre of the lake. Finally, Ernie untied the tow rope and rowed back to the wharf.

We all watched as the pilot taxied back and forth a few times and then stiffened nervously as the seaplane effortlessly roared up off the lake.

What a beautiful sight!

We all cheered as the pilot flew back and forth twice more before landing the plane again and re-anchoring at the wharf with Ernie's help. The pilot clambered out of the cockpit, stepped down onto a pontoon, and from there climbed the ladder onto the wharf. Then he warmly shook Blackie's hand.

"Blackie," he said, "you did a great job. Thank you! I'm

back in business thanks to your great skill in repairing aircraft engines!"

"Well," said Blackie smugly, "a seaplane is only an automobile with wings and pontoons. Not a big deal."

Later, after the plane was reloaded and the surface of Seton Lake was beginning to get choppy with waves—ideal conditions for lifting the nose and wings of a seaplane—the pilot took off again and headed westward up Seton Lake, final destination Vancouver. Blackie Blackburn grinned as he strutted back to his car, waved a friendly goodbye from his driver's-side window, and drove back to town.

My brother Allan and his companions in their Boy Scout troop had changed into swimming trunks at their camp and come back to the wharf to practise diving. Coincidently, my oldest brother, Ernie, had arrived from a fishing jaunt just as the plane headed off up the lake. He had caught nine twelve-inch rainbow trout and two eighteen-inch Dolly Varden trout. He presented the fish to Allan's Boy Scouts, myself included, for our dinner menu.

Around noon the waves began to develop whitecaps and the lake became too rough for diving or even swimming close to the wharf. A big wave could toss a swimmer violently against the wharf, fracturing a hand, a wrist, an arm, or a leg.

The waves began splashing up onto the surface of the wharf. Ernie Marshall asked some of the boys to help him to secure the mooring of the for-hire rowboats to prevent them from smashing up against the huge fir logs under the wharf. Then he asked them to help pull in the diving board plank while he carefully backed his car off its end and back onto solid ground.

In the meantime, my brother Ernie had asked me to look after his fishing rod, backpack, and other gear while he went into the bushes and changed into his swimming trunks. Back on the wharf, he added his clothing to the rest of his belongings for me to watch over. He had intended to join the others in diving practice off our impromptu diving board, but now that it was removed and the lake was rough, he sat and chatted with Allan's Boy Scouts.

Allan told his group that Ernie was a great diver and an excellent swimmer. One of his greatest skills, Allan said, was swimming long distances underwater. Ernie could hold his breath underwater at least ten seconds at a time between trips to the surface. I could swim underwater for maybe three seconds at most. I don't think Allan could do much better.

Eventually the lake got so rough that everyone got ready to leave. Then suddenly someone shouted, "Listen! Someone is out on the lake calling for help!"

We all stopped what we were doing and listened carefully.

"There!" Ernie Marshall shouted. "It's coming from over there near Yellow Point! Sounds like a woman's voice. Can't you hear it?" He indicated a spot about a quarter mile up on the south side of the lake.

"No," said my brother, "but I can see her now, wearing a yellow bathing cap. Right in front of us, about one hundred yards out. There, she yelled again! She's calling for help! You must have heard her that time. I wonder who in hell would go swimming in Seton Lake this time of the day. God, how stupid can you get?"

"Someone get a rowboat. Row out and get her before she gets too tired and drowns!"

"You can't row a boat in this kind of water," Ernie Marshall yelled. "She's a goner!"

But my brother Ernie was already in the water. I could see him about ten feet from the wharf, swimming rapidly beneath the surface toward the stricken swimmer.

"There he goes. Under the water! Don't you see him?" I shouted, pointing.

Everyone fell silent. Finally, Ernie's head came up for air, and everyone shouted at once, "I see him! I see him!"

"He'll never make it in time," said someone.

"Yes, he can! He can do it!" I screamed as loudly as I could over the noise of the waves.

All of us were holding our breath. Someone was reciting the Lord's Prayer. I cheered, "Hooray!" whenever Ernie's head appeared over the top of a wave. He rapidly progressed, swimming underwater and bobbing up for a quick breath now and then.

And I must admit that I was worried, but it didn't take Ernie very long to cover the one hundred yards. And finally I saw his head right beside hers, and I knew he would save her.

"He made it!" I shouted to the people around me on the wharf. "He's got her. She'll be okay now."

I knew Ernie would talk to her, ask her to calm down, and tell her that if she relaxed and floated on her back, he could tow her safely to shore.

We all watched with bated breath as the two heads got closer and closer to shore, until Ernie stood up waist high in the water, turned sideways and gently pushed her body up onto the beach where she lay with her head and shoulders out of the water. I could see her still gasping for breath, but I knew she would be okay.

I suddenly felt tears welling up in my eyes. So I crept over to a corner of Ernie Marshall's boathouse tool shed, leaned against the wall, put my head down, and burst into tears. My body was racked with sobs. I couldn't help it. I had to cry.

Neve Pizzi heard me, saw where I had gone, and rushed to my rescue, pushing her way through the noisy crowd. She put her arms around me and pressed me to her bosom until I stopped crying. I was an emotional wreck.

Meanwhile several women had rushed across the beach to the woman who lay, half in, half out of the water. They lifted her onto an air mattress and covered her with a warm blanket. The woman had tears in her eyes as she said in a low voice, "I'll be all right after I rest for a while. Can someone please go over to Craig Lodge and ask my husband, Mr. Hitchens, to come and get me?" And please bring my saviour to me right now! Bring me the brave young man who risked his life. I want to thank him for saving me from drowning. I had no idea that the lake could get so rough. Those waves were so tiring. I thought I was going to die. I thought I was going to go under for sure, and then that wonderful young man appeared. Someone up there must have been watching over me and sent an angel to rescue me."

Ernie told me years later that the woman was so grateful that she wanted him to come to Vancouver and live with her and her family. She said that she would send him to university or do whatever he wanted to help him get an education. Maybe she wanted to adopt him. Who knows?

No mention was made of Ernie's heroism in the local *Bridge River Lillooet News*. And no one stopped me on the street and said, "You must be proud of your brother." Perhaps the townsfolk were of the opinion that Ernie should be thankful that he had been chosen by fate and given the opportunity to do such a public deed. Perhaps they believed that saving a life in such a circumstance was the least one of his class could do to pay for the privilege of living in the town. Bertie Craig asked me one afternoon, when I was standing on our lower-class wharf across from the lodge, to tell my brother that he was very, very, impressed with what Ernie had done.

Two years later, Craig Lodge was suddenly shut down. Workmen from Vancouver appeared on the scene shortly after, tore it down, and loaded the pieces onto a PGE flatcar. I heard through the grapevine that all the salvageable material was taken away to Squamish. The train station, too, was demolished soon afterwards.

I sought out Tom Manson one Saturday morning, as he sat alone on the bench in front of Billy Taverna's barbershop, and asked him why it was torn down. Tom said he'd known the lodge would eventually have to close down and go belly up, because it never was a safe place for tourists. "Those damned fools built that big expensive lodge right at the foot of a big Talus slope, a natural rock slide. A goat or a deer crossing at the top of the slide, even a human sneeze or a bird breaking wind, could start a rock rolling down the slope. And it would pick up a lotta speed on the way down."

"Anyone who's ever visited Seton Lake remembers hearing rocks roaring down from the top of the slope onto the PGE railroad tracks from time to time. They made one helluva noise when they came down the mountainside and kicked up quite a cloud of dust. Some of those rocks were a foot in diameter, big enough to kill ten men."

"Tom Taylor," he went on, "used to ride out on his pump-handled handcar to check the slide every morning and give the PGE cleanup crew time to clear the tracks before the freight or passenger trains came by later. Well, some of those rocks started going through the walls of the lodge and scared the hell outta people! Tourists naturally stopped coming. Who in his right mind wants to sleep in a bed when a rock might come smashing through the wall beside him? So Craig Lodge went broke!"

Boy scout camping trip, Seton Lake, 1935: Gordon, Clifford, &
the Larder twins. Allan is on the right.

Children swimming in Seton Lake, 1970.

Joanne looking towards the site of the defunct Craig Lodge.

TWENTY

FISHING

This story is fictional, but as a child, I always wished some enterprising girl would venture down to the creek and allow me to share my fishing passion and expertise. As I got older, I did accompany a few girls on fishing expeditions. Here, Hazel Arthur—my good friend and classmate —stands in for them. This is how I imagined our fishing adventures would have played out.

"Why are you following me?" I spoke over my shoulder to the girl on the creek bank behind me. It was a warm spring afternoon, and I was fishing for grayling. The creek was noisy, but I heard strange noises behind me. On the alert, I immediately looked behind me to check. Maybe it was another pesky black bear.

It wasn't a bear. It was a girl.

I recognized her immediately, despite her boyish attire. She was in my Grade 7 class, and I saw her every day at school. I knew her name, too—Hazel Arthur—but I'd never spoken to her in class or at recess, and she had never spoken to me. She was always surrounded by other girls, and girls and boys didn't hang out together. I had a few friends, boys and girls in Grade 5, with whom I chummed around at school. They were ten like me, but I had been skipped two grades in school and found myself two or three years younger than anyone else in my class. Hazel, I guessed, was twelve or thirteen.

Hazel was clever, bright, and always had her hand up to answer questions put to the class by Miss MacLelland, our teacher. She was plain-looking but cute, and always prettily dressed, often in pleated Highland skirts and colourful blouses, pink or sometimes blue to match her large blue eyes. In winter she wore heavy woollen slacks and a hooded melton cloth jacket for outside wear. Inside the schoolroom, it was again skirts and blouses or whatever else girls wore.

I knew by her clothing alone that she was from a well-to-do family. Her father, Fred Arthur, worked for the PGE Railway. And I knew she had three brothers. The oldest went to the University of British Columbia. (In a small town, everyone knew something about everyone else, at least by name. It was common gossip—"the popular pastime," my mother said.)

I was part of the poor class, the "reliefers," as we were called in town. I lived in a shack on the Cayoosh Creek flats. Every school kid from the upper class knew that I was from the other side of the railroad tracks. (That expression didn't make any sense to me because, in Lillooet, the other side of the railroad tracks was either gravel banks, bushes, creek, or forest. No one lived near the PGE tracks, no matter which side of a fence they were on.)

Anyway, I'd never seen Hazel in blue jeans, a boy's shirt, and running shoes before. Why, I wondered, was she was standing on the bank on Sunday morning, dressed like a boy?

I looked over my right shoulder to see if I could spot other people on the creek bank. She was alone. It was strange, a girl from a well-to-do family, following me while I fished in Cayoosh Creek a mile from town. Didn't she know that it was dangerous for a young girl to wander unaccompanied by a brother, a father, an uncle? To me, "dangerous" meant that she could get lost, fall in the creek and drown, or get bitten by a stray dog or black bear—of which there were many, raiding garbage cans and orchards. One bear even followed me one day when I was fishing, hoping to get a free meal of rainbow trout, I guessed. What if the bear had made a run at me while I was landing a fish? Where could I have gone? Into the creek? Up a tree? Bears can climb trees too!

I shouted above the wind, "Is that you, Hazel? What are you doing here? Are you following me?"

Her answer came immediately. "Who says I'm following you? Why would I be following you? It's a free country, isn't it?"

Just like a girl, I thought, but I knew that some girls could talk that way to boys. "Well, you're not fishing. Where's your fishing pole?"

Hazel slid down the gravel bank and walked gingerly over to where I was standing with my fishing rod in my hand.

"I haven't got one yet," Hazel said, a little out of breath, "but I'm going to. Maybe you could help me get one. You're so clever at everything in school. So why not out of school too?"

"Well," I said, "I'm not good at everything out of school."

"Everyone in our class knows you're really good at fishing. I guess I feel jealous of you, a boy, being better at something ordinary like fishing."

"Fishing isn't ordinary," I said. "It's special, and it takes a lot of time to learn how to do it."

"Why can't girls be taught how to fish?" retorted Hazel. "I asked my dad to teach me, but he says he's too busy. I know he knows how to fish. So I decided to visit you and ask you to teach me how."

"How did you find me?" I asked.

"I came down Station Hill and went to your shack on the creek. Nobody answered my knock, so I called out your name three times and even went down the path from your door that leads to the creek. I could see the bridge from there, but I couldn't see you anywhere on the creek bank, so I took a chance and walked up the path along the creek toward the

O'Donaghy house. I spotted you right here, fishing on the creek, and here I am."

I smiled at her. She was brave for a girl, coming down to the Cayoosh Creek flats all by herself, but I felt uneasy. I'd never even heard of a girl who liked fishing.

She stood hesitantly, even timidly, beside me, watching me cast my grasshopper-baited hook into the creek, letting it drift downstream and around a big rock into a pool. I did this several times before retrieving my line and turning to confront Hazel, who stood smiling up at me in obvious admiration. She was fascinated by my technique, the adroit handling of my homemade rod. "You make it look so easy," she said. "Is there a trout hiding in that pool?"

"There could be," I said, "and maybe he's not hungry, or maybe he isn't even there. Maybe he has found a better feeding spot in another pool."

"Gordon, why don't you help me make a fishing rod and teach me how to catch a rainbow trout? I really want to learn to fish. My mom is always teasing me, calling me a tomboy, but she buys me blue jeans and doesn't mind a bit if I dress and act a bit like a boy. Of course, I play girls' games with my girlfriends. But I want to learn how to fish. Don't some girls, some women, know how to fish? Girls ride bikes. And Mrs. Jones teaches girls to ride horses down on Jones's ranch. She says in England, even the queen and princesses ride horses."

I interrupted her. "Why should I help you get a rod and teach you how to fish? You girls aren't really interested in fishing, are you? Don't you play with dolls and make-believe tea parties? What would you do with a fishing pole? And who says I'm clever at everything out of school? And it's Sunday! Why aren't you in Sunday school?"

She ignored my questions. "Maybe you could teach me how to catch fish. My cousin, Chuck, is always bragging about the fish he catches. I think I could catch a fish if I had the opportunity."

I pondered for a second over the word *opportunity*. Did she mean *chance*? And if she meant *chance*, why say another word, like *o-p-p-o-r-t-u-n-i-t-y*? And was that how you spelled it, with two p's?

"I didn't know Chuck liked fishing. I've never seen him fishing down here on the creek or out at the lake. Anyway, why doesn't he teach you how to fish?" I asked.

"Chuck only fishes in Pine Lake," said Hazel, "and that's miles away up the PGE rail line, on the way to Pavilion Mountain. My Uncle Pete drops off Chuck and his brother Ray from the PGE work train on Saturday mornings, so they can fish at Pine Lake. Then he brings them back Sunday night. You knew that Chuck's dad is a conductor on the PGE work train, didn't you? Chuck brings home quite a few trout, and my mom cooks them for all of us for Monday night supper."

"What kind of trout are they—rainbows, browns, or brookies?" I asked.

"I don't know one fish from another. Chuck just calls them lake trout," said Hazel.

"Why doesn't Ray's mother cook the trout for his family?" I mused out loud.

Hazel answered, "He and Ray had a mother, but she doesn't live with them anymore. Chuck never talks about her. I think she left their dad for another man she met at the community hall Saturday dance a year ago. It's a big secret. Don't tell anyone I told you all this. My mother says I'm not to bother myself with town gossip. Leave that to grown-ups, she says!"

"I bet Chuck would show you how to fish if you asked him," I said.

"I don't want Chuck to teach me anything," Hazel replied. "I don't like Chuck. I never have, and I never will!"

"He's your cousin, part of your family. You should like him, shouldn't you?"

"No," said Hazel heatedly, "I shouldn't have to like anyone

I don't like. Why can't we pretend that you're my cousin, Gordon?"

"People don't pretend things about cousins," I said.

"Are you afraid of having a girl cousin? Are you afraid of girls? Are you afraid of me?" she said with a malicious grin.

"What?" I said. "Afraid of you? No, I'm not afraid of you. I'm just not used to being around girls. Boys don't play with girls. And maybe I am afraid of a girl who follows a boy when he's fishing, because girls don't fish. Why are you following me? Why are you watching me? Are you spying on me? Did somebody send you to spy on me?"

"Well," replied Hazel, "I guess I am spying on you. Joey Hurley said you taught his cousin Bobby to fish, even going up to the bottom of the Falls twice last year with your brother Allan looking after you and keeping you two out of danger. I don't want to ever go near any falls. It sounds terribly dangerous. I'm not brave like you are, Gordon. But Joey said that Bobby is crazy about fishing. He even has his dad drive him out to Seton Lake so he can practise fishing for squaw fish off the wharf."

"Nobody eats squaw fish," I said with a note of disgust in my voice. "Why does Bobby want to catch squaw fish when there are rainbow trout just a short hike down Seton Creek from the parking lot at the wharf? I saw Joey's dad fishing there quite a few times in the early evening last summer. I think he drives out after coming home from work at five o'clock. I've seen his car parked at the wharf several times. I don't know whether or not he has any luck, but they say there are big wild rainbows in that part of Seton Creek."

"Well," said Hazel, "maybe Bobby wants to practise on squaw fish before trying to catch a big rainbow fish."

"Don't say *rainbow fish*!" I admonished her. "Say *rainbow trout.*"

"Okay, okay, rainbow trout, rainbow trout, rainbow trout,"

laughed Hazel. She seemed extremely happy that I was at least talking to her about fishing.

I grinned at her and said, "Well, maybe I could try to teach you how to fish in Cayoosh Creek, but you'd have to realize you'd be in a lot of danger. Creeks and lakes and rivers are dangerous places for careless people. Accidents are always waiting to happen, and people like you and me, right here on the creek, can drown if they simply don't know how to wade safely in the swift, flowing water."

"You know Mr. Manson — Tom Manson — don't you? He lives near here, on the west bank of the Fraser at the foot of Station Hill. He taught me how to fish for freshwater ling cod in his lagoon at the north end of his orchard. He told me before I started fishing — that was when I was eight — that whenever you play around with water, especially fast-flowing creek water and, even worse, fast-flowing Fraser River water, you are in danger. You can drown if you're not careful."

I could see that my words had begun to frighten Hazel, so I quickly added, "But don't worry, Hazel, I'll teach you how to fish in perfect safety." She relaxed, and a faint smile reappeared, replacing the wide grin that had stretched across her freckled face a few moments before.

"There's a good example," I said, pointing. "See the island in front of us? I usually fish in the big bright green pool at its lower end. You can just see the top end of the pool peeking out from behind the big, white granite boulder. Can you see it?"

"Yes, I can see it," said Hazel, "It's a pretty colour. Bright green, not pale green like the water here."

"I think it's because the water there is calm and deep," I said. "Deep water is always bright green in Cayoosh Creek. Maybe Miss MacLelland knows why Cayoosh Creek water is green, and maybe she knows, too, why Seton Lake water is sky blue."

"Let's ask her in our next science class," said Hazel.

"Yes, let's," I said.

We both stared in silence at the island for several minutes.

"Now," I went on, "try to guess: how could we ever cross over to the island when you can see, right in front of us, at least twenty-five feet of fast-flowing creek water between us and the island?"

Hazel didn't know, so she remained silent.

"We'd have to wade, and just to show you how dangerous it can be, take my hand and we'll step a few feet into the creek and feel the strength of the cold current on our legs. Don't worry about your pant legs getting wet. They will quickly dry out. And don't worry about your fancy running shoes. They will get wet, but they will protect your feet from sharp stones, so you won't stumble and fall down in the creek. And remember: we mustn't ever lose our footing and fall down into the water."

"Hold my hand, Gordie," Hazel cried. "I'm afraid!"

"That's a good sign," I said as I firmly held her warm hand. "Fear is a good warning sign that tells us to be careful. If we ever feel that the current is beginning to lift our feet off the creek bottom, we'll have to get back out of the water and find a quieter spot in which to wade, or we could be swept downstream and drown. If you hit your head on a stone and become unconscious, you will drown. And, as Tom Manson says, you can drown in two inches of water if your face is under the water and you can't fill your lungs with air. Then it's game over, unless someone rescues you immediately and drains the water out of your lungs."

"I'm not going to show you that place where I wade out to the island. That'd be too much work for a first lesson. Besides, that's my secret way of keeping people from fishing on the island. I'll show you how to fish in a safe spot just downstream. You won't have to wade at all, and we can concentrate on learning how to bait the hook with a grasshopper and how to cast your line into a small pool where I usually get a bite."

She followed close behind me as I made my way carefully

from one large, dry stone to another until we came to where Cayoosh Creek made a sharp left turn toward its mouth in the Fraser River. We could just see the north end of the car bridge where it crossed over the creek about a hundred yards downstream.

"Did you notice," I said, "how I avoided stepping on wet stones?"

Hazel nodded. "Why do you avoid wet stones?"

"Because wet stones can be slippery. And wet logs can be slippery too. Always try to walk on dry things. You mustn't slip and lose your footing, or you'll get hurt. Or maybe you'll drop your fishing rod and damage or lose it. Did you notice that I carry my rod in my left hand when I'm walking? That's because I'm right-handed. I need my right hand free to grab onto things for support."

"I'm right-handed too," replied Hazel proudly.

I suddenly poked the butt end of my homemade fishing rod toward her left hand and said, "Here, hold my rod the same way I was holding it." Hazel carefully clutched the butt end of my fishing rod, but in her haste to comply, she mistakenly grasped the rod in her right hand.

I reached out, gently uncurled the tightened fingers of her right hand, and placed the end of the rod back into her left hand. "There, that's better. You forgot for a moment what I said about keeping your right hand free for support. And if you get tired, you can always sit on a log, catch your breath, and have a look around. The point is to be careful and move slowly."

"Sometimes, Hazel, you have to move through bush. If you do, you can use your right hand to separate the branches and make space for your rod. Never let go of your rod, and never bump it or let it be damaged."

I could see she needed a rest, so I sat on the nearby log and patted a spot beside me. "Do you like learning how to fish so far?" I asked.

She nodded and leaned against me as if for support.

"We haven't even got to actually do any fishing yet," I said.

Hazel sat beside me and smiled. She proudly held up her left hand to show me that she was clutching the rod the way I had just taught her. It was almost like a show of affection for me as her teacher. Or just pride of achievement.

"Now," I said, "look back and see how far we have walked already, stepping on dry rocks. Never once did you lose your grip on the rod. You are a very careful person, Hazel. I think you are going to be good at fishing."

Hazel looked up at me the way a new pupil looks at a teacher. "I think, Gordon, with you as my teacher, I will really become good at fishing. And won't Mom and Dad be proud if someday I can come home with trout for Mom to cook for dinner?"

"Well, you are a good listener," I said, "and if you carefully follow my instructions, you will become an expert fishing girl. You will never have an accident, never fall into the water, and you'll catch a lot of fish. I'll make it much easier for you to learn, and I'll never, ever, take you into danger—like my two older brothers did when they showed *me* how to fish." I sighed. "The easy part with them was learning to hold my fishing rod, to catch grasshoppers, to put a grasshopper on a hook. The scariest part of their lesson included crossing over a very dangerous, narrow path cut into the clay bluff just upstream from the O'Donaghy house. Hazel, I was scared to death, but I made it safely by closely following their instructions, listening to where they told me to place my feet on the path, and never once looking down at the deep green water twenty feet below. I was afraid of falling into the creek and drowning. Just imagine, Hazel: they were fourteen and sixteen, and I was only eight at the time! Now, here I am, at ten, showing you how to fish. How old are you?" I asked.

"I'm twelve, but I'll soon be thirteen," Hazel replied. Then, looking up at me admiringly, she remarked, "Gordon, I find it hard to believe you are only ten. With the way you explain things, you must be at least as old as I am. And you are as tall as I am and much stronger that I will ever be."

"I guess boys are stronger than girls, but you look strong. You look like you have muscles. And I have seen how fast you can run on Sports Day. You are lucky you are a girl. Girls are prettier than boys, and you can always wear pretty clothes to school. Just look at me. I'm always dressed like a bum. I don't have nice-looking clothes except for the one shirt and necktie I wear to Sunday school Bible class."

"You always look okay at the monthly school dance," Hazel assured me.

"I guess so," I murmured, "but it's the same shirt and tie I wear to Sunday school. Most of the time I wear hand-me-downs. My mother and my grandmother are good at sewing and knitting and patching. My granny makes nice patchwork quilts out of all kinds of old clothes—old coats, mainly, that richer people are tired of wearing and donate to the Salvation Army centre. Nothing is ever thrown away in my grandmother's house, or in our own shack either. I even know how to darn my socks when they get holes in their toes. I use an old burnt-out light bulb, a big darning needle, and matching wool yarn. I'm good at darning."

"Do you have electricity in your house?" Hazel asked in astonishment.

"No way," I said. "Only rich people can afford to have their houses wired for electricity."

"Then where did you get a burnt-out light bulb?"

"From the town garbage dump down by the Fraser River," I replied. "I get lots of stuff rich people throw away in the dump."

"What do you use for light in your shack at night?" Hazel asked.

"We use kerosene lamps or candles."

"Gee, we have electricity in our house," said Hazel matter-of-factly. "And when a bulb burns out, we just put it in the garbage."

"Lucky you," I said. "Next time I need a bulb for darning socks, can I get one from your garbage can?"

"Sure you can," she said with a big smile. "I'll even save a new one for you. Then you'll have one to spare just in case you ever need another."

"Thanks, Hazel," I said. "That will save me a trip to the town dump. But when I grow up," I went on seriously, "I'm gonna have a home that's wired up for electricity. There'll be no more kerosene lamps for me! Down here on the Cayoosh flats, we have to use a kerosene lamp—or coal oil lamp, as some people call them—for reading, cooking, and washing up. It's made of glass and nice to look at with its tall glass chimney. But if it's dropped or knocked over, it can start a fire and burn down your shack in no time at all. Have you seen a kerosene lamp before?"

"I don't think so," Hazel said.

"Most people in the olden days," I continued, "had to use candles for light in their homes at night. And candles can be dangerous and start a fire. Electricity is really safe. However, a candle can be fun when you use it to make a bug. A bug is a homemade lantern for night use. My brothers showed me how to make one. I could make one for you sometime and show you how to use it at night. All you need is a candle and an empty lard pail. With a bug, I have a lot of fun walking around outside at night, pretending I'm a lightning bug."

"Maybe," Hazel offered, "you can come visit me some evening and make me a bug?"

"Yeah," I replied. "I could get the materials, an empty lard pail, some wire for a handle, and a candle. I'd need a hammer, a spike, and some other tools. Does your dad have a workshop, or a few tools, maybe?" I asked with enthusiasm.

"Yes, he does, in our basement," Hazel said, "but I can't

make things like you can, Gordon. I'll have to just watch you make it. You are so clever at everything!"

"Yeah, well," I said, "maybe I am. A bit, anyway." Feeling a little embarrassed, I said, "Lets continue with the fishing lesson."

We got off the driftwood log we'd been sitting on, and I picked up my fishing rod and led Hazel down toward the bend in the creek. I walked toward a particularly large creek boulder and stopped just before we reached it. I could see that behind the boulder was quite a nice pool, deep enough to hide a rainbow trout big enough to keep: eight inches long, according to the law.

As we got within ten feet of the boulder, I motioned for Hazel to stoop beside me and creep forward. "Don't talk or make any noise, especially with your feet," I cautioned. "Trout are easily scared, and they are always on guard. If a fish sees us, it will dive immediately to the bottom of the pool and stay hidden for quite a while. Also, we have to stoop, so we won't be silhouetted against the sky. But we don't have to creep right to the very edge of the pool because my fishing rod is about six feet long. We can stop that far from the pool's edge. From there I can easily cast my line right into the pool without the trout seeing a thing until my grasshopper hits the water."

When we were in position, I shifted my rod from my left hand to my right. With a loop of line dangling loosely from my left hand, I showed Hazel where to stand, about three feet away on my left side, so she could watch everything I did. Then, holding the loop of line up off the rocks so the hook wouldn't snag on a rock or a piece of driftwood, I pointed my rod tip toward the pool and flicked it into the air and toward the centre of the creek. The extra line and the baited hook followed behind it. "This is called casting," I said.

When the grasshopper bait was passing over the spot I wanted, I quickly lowered my right wrist, bringing the rod tip down to the horizontal so that the grasshopper plopped onto the water, the extra line dropping onto the water too. Hazel and I both watched as the line and the bait swirled around on the top of the pool for a minute, until the grasshopper started to sink out of sight.

"Watch the grasshopper, Hazel," I said. "If it sinks out of sight, don't give up. Watch the floating line instead. If the line starts to twitch, that means that a trout is trying to swallow the grasshopper. To do so, it has to tug on my line. So when I guess that the trout has the bait in its mouth, I can pull up hard with my right hand, lift the line, set the hook in the trout's mouth, jerk the fish out of the water, and drop it on the ground beside me.

"If the trout doesn't come out of the water, I'll know I didn't properly hook it. But if a trout does, I can swing it high toward you, over my left shoulder, and right onto the rocks. If I have been lucky, there it will be: a big trout wriggling on the ground, flipping up and down and trying to get back into the pool. I'll have to be quick, put down my rod, and rush over to grab the trout with both hands before it has a chance to get away."

I put my hand on her trembling arm and said soothingly, "Don't be upset, Hazel, by the complicated steps you will have to go through. Later, we can practise the whole thing on dry land. We don't need a pool, and we don't need a grasshopper. We'll use a piece of a lead sinker instead. And we can practise in your front yard, if that's okay."

"Gee, that'll be okay," said Hazel.

"Now, come and stand on my right side, so we can try something a bit different," I said.

Hazel followed my instruction and was soon at my side.

"Put your right hand on top of my right hand, and I will go through the motions again, so you can get the feel of what I'm doing. Don't worry about my left hand for now. Just concentrate on my right hand."

I cast several times with Hazel clutching the wrist of my

right hand in her own. I said, "Did you feel how my right hand cast the rod and the line forward?"

"Yes, I think I did," said Hazel.

"I know you couldn't see the line as it slipped through my left hand, but when I let it go free, did you see it fly out over the pond and fall into the water, along with the grasshopper?"

"Yes, I think I saw that," said Hazel.

"At the end of each cast, I retrieved the line with the grasshopper by raising the tip of my rod from horizontal over the pool to a vertical position right above my head. Could you see the line and the grasshopper lift up off the water and swing through the air toward us? Did you see me catch the line in my left hand?"

"Yes, yes, I saw all that," said Hazel excitedly.

"Well," I said apologetically, "you couldn't see what my left hand was doing all that time, with its palm open and ready to catch the line as it came off the water and swung through the air toward us. But now we'll work on that."

I was hoping that at least she had gotten the feel of casting and retrieving by holding onto my right hand. I had never before tried to teach anyone, especially a girl, how to bait cast, and it worried me. But with forced enthusiasm, I said, "Now it's time for you to get the feeling of what I was doing with my left hand all this time. So I want you to keep holding my right wrist but reach behind my back and put your left hand on top of my left wrist."

It was a stretch for Hazel to reach across my back, so she resorted to piggybacking me, putting her arms around my neck and leaning forward to maintain her tight grip on my right wrist. It was as if she were trying to give me a really big bear hug.

It was too much for me. I staggered a little, on the verge of collapsing. I knew I would have to ask Hazel to get off my back. But she suddenly collapsed backward onto the ground, roaring with laughter. I sat down beside her, laughing so hard that I too fell backwards onto the gravel. We lay there, both gasping for breath but greatly amused by what had happened.

"We both need a rest," I said, "so is it okay if we just lie here for a while?"

"Yes, let's!" gasped Hazel.

After several quiet minutes I turned my head toward Hazel and said, "We can give it another try at the pool. You can watch my left hand, and then you can try it a few times on your own while I coach you. You may find it difficult, but remember that even a lot of grown-ups have trouble learning. I will make sure that you can do it all perfectly. You will be Lillooet's first famous fisher girl."

"How did you like my bear hug?" asked Hazel with a broad grin as she sat up.

I didn't comment, but I laughed and reached out to touch her right hand. Hazel reacted by taking both my hands in hers as I got up. Then she moved gently toward me until our faces almost touched, and, smiling, kissed me lightly on my lips.

I was startled, and l moved back and let go of her hands.

"That's just my way of thanking you for agreeing to teach me how to fish," Hazel whispered. "You're not mad at me for thanking you, are you?"

"Of course not," I whispered. "Some people shake hands, and some people kiss, I guess."

"Gee, I guess I should have asked you first. In our family, we don't shake hands, we kiss."

"It's okay," I whispered again. "I'm not mad, and anyway my hands are all covered with smelly grasshopper smell. If we shook hands, I'd make you all smelly too."

"Was that the first time a girl kissed you, Gordon?" Hazel asked.

"Yes," I said uncertainly. "Yes, I guess it was."

"Did you absolutely hate it?" she whispered.

"No," I said. "It felt nice. But what if someone saw us?"

"Next time," Hazel said, "I'll check to see if anyone is watching. Will that be okay?"

"Yeah, sure."

"I wonder if my mother is worried about me being absent," she said in her normal voice. "Could you walk me home up Station Hill? My mother could make hot chocolate. And she makes great cookies."

"Yeah, I can," I said, "and we can pass by my shack on the way. That's near where I want to teach you the next lesson in bait casting."

Hazel looped her arm in mine as we walked along, and I didn't object. But my right hand gripped the butt of my rod a bit more tightly as we moved along toward my shack.

When we got to the door, I carefully placed my pole and line and grasshopper on two nails driven into the wall between the door and the window. Then I unlocked the door with a key from my pocket and beckoned Hazel inside. But after a quick look I stepped back outside and closed the door behind me. "My mother and brother are uptown visiting the Jim family. Did your parents know where you were going today?"

"I told them I was going for a walk with Peggy Dowson down to the Cayoosh Creek Bridge and back so we could write a paragraph to bring to school on Monday. We need to write about the frogs that live in the pond at the foot of Station Hill. Some people say the frogs chirp all night long in summer."

"And what will your parents say if they find out that you were fibbing? Won't your mom ask to see the paragraph before you leave for school in the morning?"

"Well," Hazel went on, "you could tell me about the frogs on the way up to my house, and then I could easily write the paragraph tonight and show it to my mom in the morning before I leave for school."

Stepping out onto the gravel flat, I pointed to the hill a hundred yards north and the narrow path that zigzagged down the face of the hill. It started at a notch cut into the town flat at the top of the path. "That's the shortcut I come down every day from school," I told her. I explained that I went to school up Station Hill but returned by the shortcut from the flat on which Hazel's house was located, behind the PGE railroad tracks. "Did you come down that path or did you walk down Station Hill this morning?" I asked.

"I didn't know there was a path there," said Hazel. "I walked down Station Hill."

"If it's okay with you, we can go up to your house by climbing up the path instead." I looked down at her running shoes. "But your shoes may get quite dirty on the path."

"Let's use the path," said Hazel. "My shoes don't matter. Besides, there's a lot of dust from passing cars on Station Hill."

So we climbed the path and emerged onto the upper flat just two hundred feet south of the railroad tracks. Looking back, Hazel said, "What a view! You are lucky, Gordon, to live on such a beautiful creek. Next time I come to you for more lessons, I want to come this way instead of down Station Hill."

"That's okay," I said, "but whichever way you choose, I will come and pick you up and bring you down here. You mustn't ever come by yourself."

Hazel nodded her head in silent agreement. "My mother will like that because she worries about me all the time. Can we tell her all about the first lesson you gave me today, so I can get permission for you to give me more?"

"That's a really good idea," I said as we crossed the railroad tracks, "but what about your dad? Will he let you come down to the Cayoosh and take lessons from me? Will he be worried about you falling in the creek? Would he mind having you come home smelling of fish and grasshoppers? And will it be okay for you to spend so much time alone with me, without any adult supervising? Maybe he could come and watch me teach you if he is worried about your safety."

"Sure," said Hazel. "We can tell them both what we did today, and what you told me about being so very careful while fishing on the creek. And we can tell them not to worry, that you're my new boyfriend."

"Is telling them I'm your boyfriend such a good idea, Hazel?" I said. "Aren't we all supposed to be just friends because we're all together in the same class?"

"Yes," said Hazel, "we're all friends when we are in Miss MacLelland's class, and she is sort of like a mother to all of us students."

"Does being your boyfriend mean that we would have to talk to each other in school every day too?"

"Wouldn't you like to talk to me at school?" asked Hazel. "Couldn't we talk about fishing?"

"Well, I'm not sure," I replied. "Isn't a boy talking to a girl like being a serious boyfriend? Like the boys in the senior grades do?"

"No, no, no!" said Hazel, stopping and stamping her feet. She glared at me. "We'll just be like ordinary friends, and ordinary friends are allowed to talk in school, aren't they?"

"I guess so, but will we have to hold hands like Beulah and Joey?"

"Not when there are other people around," said Hazel reassuringly. "But why can't we when there are no people around?"

"Okay! But what about when you have to thank me for something. Do we have to kiss?"

"Only if there isn't anyone watching," said Hazel. "Would that be okay?"

"Yeah, I guess so," I said with a puzzled grin on my averted face. I found it disturbing to look directly into Hazel's bright blue eyes. She seemed to look right through me.

We stopped walking and stood against the fence under the lowering branches of an apricot tree in front of Mr. Jack Purdy's house. "I wonder what time it is now?" asked Hazel.

I looked up into the sky, my face shaded by the visor on my cap. "It's around noon. I can tell because the sun is at its highest."

"We're just a few minutes from my house," said Hazel. "Let's go in and tell Mother all the interesting things I've learned this morning about fishing."

Soon we were in the Arthur family's kitchen, where Mrs. Arthur was sitting over a cup of tea, reading the *Bridge River Lillooet News*. "Hi, Mom," said Hazel. "Look who I brought with me. It's Gordon, the boy I told you about."

"Well," said Mrs. Arthur, "this is a nice surprise." She put down the newspaper. "Come and sit at the table while I pour you each a cup of tea and find some cookies. Hazel, why don't you tell me all that happened to you this morning. You said you and Peggy were going to do some research on frogs that live in the pond at the foot of Station Hill. Why isn't Peggy with you now?"

Hazel explained that Peggy, for some unknown reason, hadn't rendezvoused with her, so she had gone down to call on me on the Cayoosh flats. Hazel then described our fishing lesson, leaving out the part where I had piggybacked her and we had fallen onto the gravel. "Gordon has promised to make me my own fishing rod, so I can practise bait casting for rainbow trout on our front lawn before our second lesson on the creek."

"How wonderful," said Hazel's mother.

"And Gordon said he can give me more lessons in the nice big pool under the Cayoosh Creek car bridge at the bottom of Station Hill next weekend. Will that be all right, Mom?"

"Of course," said Hazel's mother. "Your father can drive you down to the bridge in the car."

"That won't be necessary, Mrs. Arthur," I broke in. "I can very easily pick up Hazel and take her back down my zigzag shortcut path to the Cayoosh flats. We just now came up that path, and Hazel really enjoyed the climb and the view from the top. She said she could see right down on the Cayoosh Creek Bridge and then look back over her shoulder at your house too."

Mrs. Arthur nodded her agreement. As we sat and enjoyed the tea and cookies, she asked me all about school. I was very happy to oblige. "I really like school," I said. "I like learning new things, being in the classroom with all the other kids, all the nice desks, the big blackboards, the white chalk, and the coloured chalk too."

Mrs. Arthur beamed at me as I went on and on.

"Miss MacLelland even lets me take the blackboard brushes behind the building after school," I said, "and bang the chalk dust out of them. And she lets me clean off the blackboards with a damp cloth until they are shiny and black again, ready for the next day."

"That is perfectly wonderful, Gordon," said Mrs. Arthur.

"I really like school," I said softly. "I want to go to university some day and become a high school teacher myself. Maybe I was meant to be a teacher. Look how much I enjoyed teaching Hazel her first lesson in bait casting this morning. Miss MacLelland herself said I should become a professor after I finish high school. I wonder what subject I would teach if I became a professor."

"Maybe you could teach bait casting," said Hazel with a grin.

"Hazel, behave yourself," said her mother. "Gordon is serious about becoming a teacher. I can tell by the tone in his voice."

"That's okay," I said. "Hazel likes to make fun of me. Everybody in our class at school says I'm too serious about everything."

"Gee, I'm sorry, Gordon," said Hazel, "But you are so very serious in school. I have tried to talk to you at recess many times, but you are so shy. And during the lesson, you won't even look at me, and I sit right across from you in class. Mother, you should have been there this morning down on Cayoosh Creek. He kept warning me over and over about falling into the water, bumping my head on a rock, and drowning and everything."

"I don't know anything about fishing," said Hazel's mother, "but I've sat on the bank a few times and watched your father wading out into Seton Creek in his hip waders, casting his line in water that looked too deep for wading. I was worried about him then, and I'm worried about you, Hazel. I'm glad Gordon is aware of the dangers to a young girl so crazy about learning to fish."

"Mrs. Arthur, please don't worry about Hazel's safety," I said. "I was taught how to fish by my two older brothers when I was only eight — and, boy, did they ever warn me over and over about falling into the creek. And Mr. Manson, too. I remember, too, the day when Frank Vinal and Boyce Dickey were both drowned in the Fraser as they towed lumber behind their rowboat to get to their placer mine. Most of my fishing pals have a great fear of drowning, whether in Cayoosh Creek, the Fraser River, or Seton Lake. You won't see us taking chances. We spot danger when we see it, and we're always careful."

"So you see, Hazel," said Mrs. Arthur, "Gordon is only doing his duty and trying to protect you from yourself." She turned to me. "Gordon, I am glad you are going to teach Hazel how to fish. I know she will be safe with you as her teacher. I've never heard of you ever falling into Cayoosh Creek. Now, let's enjoy our tea and cookies and talk about something else."

"I'm sorry, Gordon," whispered Hazel contritely, "but you *were* very serious this morning on the creek. You almost scared me half to death at times, I was so afraid."

"That's okay," I said. "I know how it feels to be afraid."

After we had our tea with Hazel's mother and were sitting on the front porch, I said, "I have heard of quite a few drowning accidents, and I am scared too. I'm always afraid when I am around water. Tom Manson says that he, himself, is always afraid when he is around horses. He told me it's good to have a healthy fear and respect for wild horses and wild water, and wild women, too. And I guess maybe wild girls."

Mrs. Arthur supressed her laughter with her hand over her mouth at that last remark.

Hazel changed the topic. "Do you think we could practise some bait casting on our lawn now, Gordon?"

"Sure we can," I said. "But first we'll have to go to the hill behind your house and find a saskatoon bush, so I can cut off a branch with my jackknife and trim it to make you a fishing rod."

"There's a big saskatoon bush right behind our rear gate," said Hazel. "I eat saskatoon berries off it every year. Do you like saskatoons, Gordon?"

"Do I ever!" I replied. "I eat them when they are pinkish red and only half-ripe, when they are dark purple and dead ripe, and even when they are dried up like raisins. Tom Manson told me that the plains Indians of Alberta, Saskatchewan, and Manitoba used dried saskatoon berries to make pemmican before the white man came to Canada."

"What is pemmican?" Hazel asked. "I've never heard of it."

"Tom Manson says the Plains Indians mixed sundried deer meat, sundried buffalo meat, sundried saskatoon berries, and animal fat together and shaped it all into patties. Tom said that was their way of preserving meat. Then in winter, or on canoe voyages, the Indians always had meat when they couldn't get fresh game."

Hazel looked at me with adoring eyes. "Gordon, you are the smartest person I know."

I blushed. "Let's cut a saskatoon branch out back and make you a fishing rod."

An hour later I had made a rod with my jackknife, and with some twine from their kitchen and a two-inch diameter steel washer from her dad's workshop, I fashioned a suitable copy of my own bait casting gear—but without a hook and grasshopper, of course.

Out on the lawn, I demonstrated casting and retrieving twice, back and forth, back and forth, while Hazel watched. Then I handed her the rod and had her stand on the lawn away from the house with the rod in her right hand and the line and washer dangling from her left hand. She cast and retrieved several times. She looked like she had done it all her life.

"Hazel," I said, "I can hardly believe my eyes. You're what they call *a natural*! You have mastered casting and retrieving in such a very short time. I can see that I'll have to make it a bit harder for you. Just wait here until I can look around for a target."

I went to their woodpile and found a large wood chip, which I placed on the lawn about twelve feet away from her. "Pretend you are about six feet from the edge of a pool you to want fish in. I have placed the wood chip in the centre of the pretend pool. See if you can hit the wood chip with you steel washer."

After only six tries, Hazel actually hit the wood chip. I was so overcome with awe I couldn't refrain from jumping up into the air and shouting, "Perfect, perfect, perfect! Now all I have to teach you is how to catch grasshoppers. You're not afraid of grasshoppers, are you? Are you too afraid to touch a grasshopper?"

"No," she said, "I think they're cute. I watch them when they are tiny, crawling on the grass and hopping away just as I'm about to catch them. I have caught many little ones and let them go. They have such darling huge eyes, but they spit brown tobacco juice, and they can bite. I did get close to a big one out in Joe Russell's empty sagebrush lot, but they are so sneaky and so quick to hide. When I try to catch one, it always jumps and flies so high before coming back to earth. And they make their funny *k-k-k* sound as they fly."

I sat down on the veranda steps and laughed and laughed. Hazel came and sat down beside me, leaning her rod with its line and steel washer against the railing. I finally stopped laughing and looked at her admiringly. "The grasshoppers that make the *k-k-k* sound are males. Also, male grasshoppers have big, brightly coloured wings, either yellow or red. They are so beautiful! Female grasshoppers are very drab-looking, not a bit like human females. Female grasshoppers don't wear makeup. It's the male hoppers that do that," I continued, laughing.

"Why are the females drab and males so fancy?" asked Hazel.

"The drabness is for protection from predators while females are looking for a mate and especially when they are egg laying. Males' costumes are for attracting females. If you look carefully while sitting still in an empty field, you will notice dozens of big drab hoppers with swollen abdomens all around you. Those are females. If you're lucky, you will suddenly hear the *k-k-k* sound up in the sky, and if you keep absolutely still, you'll see a beautiful red-winged or yellow-winged male come down and land near you. That's what the females are waiting for. They crawl over to the male, who chooses one of them and climbs onto her back. He's her husband, and she's his wife. He then bends his tail end and locks it into her upturned tail end, so he can fertilize the ripe eggs inside her swollen abdomen. Now she is ready to lay her fertilized eggs into the sandy soil, where they will sleep all winter. The next spring, they hatch out as baby grasshoppers. The male grasshopper hops off her back and goes looking for another wife. I guess eventually he uses up all his sperm and just dies."

"Does the female die too?" asked Hazel timidly.

"Yes, she does, but only after she has buried hundreds of eggs in the soil. If you could catch a swollen female and look at her tail end, you would see her sharp digging tools called ovipositors. Camouflaged from predators, she sneaks around, finds the right kind of soil, digs a hole with her ovipositors, lays her eggs into the hole, and then covers everything with soil."

"Gee, Gordon, you are so smart. How did you learn all this stuff about grasshoppers? We didn't learn about that it in school. Miss MacLelland never told us about grasshoppers. Not one word."

"Mr. Artie Phair knows all about grasshoppers and butterflies and other insects too. You should go ask him to show you his butterfly collection. He has butterflies from all over the world. He told Clifford Jim and me all about grasshoppers after we visited his house one Saturday to look at his collection. He said that all insects do what the grasshoppers do, except each does it in its own special way. He says they are born in the spring, grow up and get married in summer, lay their eggs at the end of summer, and die in autumn. All those buried fertilized eggs that the females lay are the guarantee that there will be a new generation of grasshoppers each year. Maybe Miss MacLelland could ask Mr. Phair to come and talk to our whole class about insects."

"What do grasshopper eggs and grasshopper sperm look like?" Hazel asked.

"I don't know," I said, "but they must be awfully tiny because I could never see them no matter how hard I looked."

"And how do the grasshopper eggs and sperms turn into baby grasshoppers?"

"I don't know," I said. "Maybe your mom and dad can tell you." Then, ending the discussion, I asked, "Would you like me to pick you up and take you down to Cayoosh Creek next Sunday for a second lesson? I can take home your new rod, the one I made today, and fix it up ready for fishing. I will also have a fresh batch of grasshoppers ready for bait. Maybe you will catch some trout to bring home to your mother to cook for dinner."

"Good," said Hazel. "Wouldn't that be a wonderful surprise for my mom and my dad? What time will you come for me?"

"How about nine o'clock in the morning? Or is that too early?"

"I'll be ready long before that," said Hazel.

"Bye," I said, preparing to leave. "See you in school tomorrow morning."

"Just a minute, Gordon," Hazel said as she moved close to me. "Aren't you forgetting that I have to thank you for teaching me how to cast and for telling me all about what grasshoppers do?"

"I haven't forgotten," I said. "But is anyone watching?"

"No, I just checked," whispered Hazel. "Just move close to me and put your arms around my waist while I put my hands on your shoulders." Then she kissed me on the lips a bit more firmly than she had done on the Cayoosh flats.

Hazel followed me out to the roadway and waved as I headed for the railroad tracks and the zigzag path down the hill. I gave her a big smile and waved back.

The next day at school recess, Hazel came up to me on the playground and said, "Hi, Gordon. That was a wonderful first lesson you gave me yesterday morning down on Cayoosh Creek. You said that you can give me a second lesson next Sunday, and you mentioned you would take me to a place under the bridge."

"Yeah, that's what I thought we could do, so why don't I walk home with you today after I clean the brushes and the blackboard for Miss MacLelland? Can you wait for me in the classroom? We can talk about the lesson on the way to your house. And that's handy for me, too, because our shack is just fifteen minutes from where you live."

"I'll wait for you," said Hazel. "Is it okay if Peggy Dowson walks with us? She lives near the top of Station Hill."

"Yeah, that's okay," I said.

Next Sunday, I climbed up the zigzag path, crossed the tracks, and at nine o'clock knocked on the kitchen door of the Arthur house. Mr. Arthur answered the door and, in a very friendly voice, said, "Ah, you must be Gordon. Come on in, and I'll call Hazel. She's working with Peggy Dowson in the living room."

He went to the kitchen door and called out, "Hazel, your fishing teacher is here. Can you come to the kitchen, please?"

In a few minutes Hazel appeared, followed by her friend Peggy. "Hi, Gordon," she said. "Peggy and I are working on a school project—you know, the one about frogs. Peggy's just leaving now, and as soon as I put on my jean jacket, we can go down to the creek."

Peggy Dowson came back into the kitchen, buttoning up her coat. "Hi, Gordon. Hazel told me that you would be dropping by." She gave me a knowing smile. "So I'll let you guys go and see both at school tomorrow morning. Bye."

Soon after Peggy left, Hazel and I were at the top of the path leading down to the Cayoosh flats, and ten minutes later, we were at the Whitney shack. I took two fishing poles off the wall near the door and handed one to Hazel. I showed how I had put line on her rod that ran from where it was tied at the butt end up to the tip, where I had wound extra line and tied it with a half hitch. Then I showed her the two feet of nylon leader I had tied on the end of the line and the number-eight hook at its end.

"The nylon leader is invisible in water, so all the fish will see is the grasshopper bait," I explained. Hazel followed all I said, and as I guided her right hand, she grasped the rod in her palm, holding the line, leader, and hook between her right thumb and forefinger.

"Okay," I said, "let's walk down the creek to the pool under the Cayoosh Bridge. We'll see if you can catch a fish. I'll help you bait your hook when we get there."

When we arrived under the bridge, I leaned my rod against a big boulder and turned to Hazel. "I've already caught grasshoppers this morning." I pulled out of my shirt pocket a small matchbox containing several struggling grasshoppers. I held it up to her ear, so she could hear them scratching at the sides.

I expertly slid open one end of the matchbox and let one grasshopper stick out its head. Then I pulled that one struggling grasshopper out of the box, sliding it to shut on the rest of the grasshoppers at the same time.

"Tuck the handle of your rod under your right arm, so both hands are free. You'll need them both to put the grasshopper on your hook. With your left hand, take the grasshopper firmly out of my right hand and be careful it doesn't get away. It may try to bite you, and it might try to use its powerful hind legs to jump right out of your hand.

"With your right hand, grab the hook where it hangs at the end of the nylon leader. Then push its point into the head of the grasshopper and down through its abdomen with its point hidden inside the very tail end."

Hazel was almost able to follow my instruction, but she relaxed her grip, and the grasshopper slipped out her left hand and flew away. So I gave her another grasshopper, and this time she succeeded in properly baiting the hook.

"Now," I said, "remember what you learned about casting last Sunday. Look at the centre of the pool. Imagine there is a wood chip floating there, and try to cast the grasshopper so that it lands on that very spot."

Hazel did exactly what she was told and, surprise, surprise, immediately hooked a big rainbow trout. I grabbed her right hand and helped her jerk the trout out of the water and past her left side to land on the rocks four feet from her left shoulder. The trout frantically wriggled and flopped, trying to get back into the water. Hazel was so excited she froze, and I had to guide her over to the flip-flopping trout, making her drop her rod. I guided her hands to grip the trout securely just behind its gills.

Then I made her bang the trout's head on the nearest rock three times, so it would die.

After several minutes, I said, "Are you ready to try again? And this time, do you think you can land the trout and hit its head on a rock without any help from me?"

Hazel nodded her head and grinned. Then she stood up and got her rod ready for a second attempt.

Within an hour, Hazel had hooked five fish. Two got away, but she landed three of them, grabbing them in her hands as I had taught her and knocking their heads on a nearby stone to kill them. I added them to the other trout already in my creel.

"Hazel, that is the end of the second lesson. You don't need any more teaching, only more fishing time on the creek. Let's call it a day?" I suggested. "I'll show you how to clean the trout with my jackknife and get rid of the guts. Then we'll have to go back to your home as fast as we can and show the trout to your mom and dad. Your mom can put the trout in your refrigerator until she decides to cook them for supper."

Hazel watched as I carefully took the trout out of my creel and laid them side by side on the flat rock. Then, holding one trout firmly in my left hand and resting it on the rock, I inserted the tip of my jackknife into the trout's anus and sliced its abdomen neatly open, right up to its gills. I deftly pulled out the entrails and laid them on a nearby rock. I quickly cleaned two more and then very carefully handed Hazel the butt end of the knife and guided her through the process of eviscerating the last trout.

We both stood up and looked down proudly at the four beautiful rainbow trout. "Hazel, I'll let you dispose of the guts, so gather them up and fling them into the creek. Any other trout out there will make a good meal of them."

I put all the fish back into my leaf-lined creel and showed Hazel how to rub her hands in sand and wash them in the creek. "Now shake the water off your hands and air-dry them. Try not to get any fishy stuff on your clothing, because if you do, a wasp will smell it and immediately land on you. If that happens, don't panic, or you may get stung! Just stand still and call me. I'll remove the wasp and kill it by stepping on it on the ground."

A half hour later, we had hung our fishing poles back on the wall of the shack, climbed the path up to the town flat, and arrived at the kitchen door of Hazel's house. I took the four trout out of my creel and placed them on the plate that Hazel's mother had put on the kitchen table.

"I helped Hazel catch the first one," I said, "but she caught the other three all by herself!"

Hazel's mother gasped and went toward Hazel to give her a hug.

"Careful, Mom," said Hazel. "I smell like a fish. You'll get some fish smell on you!"

"I don't care if I do," said her mother as she hugged Hazel and kissed her on both cheeks. Then she hurried to the bottom the stairs and shouted up to her husband, "Fred, come downstairs and see the trout Hazel caught down on Cayoosh Creek."

Fred Arthur came into the kitchen, took one look at the trout and shouted, "Oh my God," I can't believe it! Are you sure Gordon didn't catch them? They are real beauties."

I turned to Hazel. "Tell them about it."

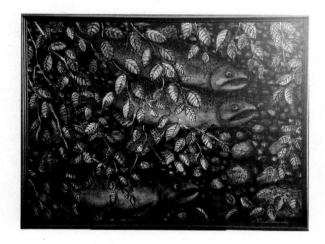

So the four of us sat down in the warm kitchen's glow, and Hazel recounted all that happened from the time she'd left home until the moment we had arrived back at the kitchen door. Hazel's parents beamed with pride as she told the story, adding a little embroidery here and there. I grinned silently with a teacher's pride during her dramatic oration.

In the weeks that followed, Hazel and I fished both sides of Cayoosh Creek, from the bridge down to the mouth of the Fraser River. We caught a lot of trout. Some were under size, and I taught her how to gently remove the hook and release the unharmed fish back into the water. I also taught her that there was a daily limit of eight fish, so we stopped fishing when together we had reached the limit. I let her do most of the fishing because I so much enjoyed watching my first and only pupil demonstrate her enthusiastic expertise.

One afternoon when Hazel and I had returned from fishing, her father went down to his workshop and returned with a gift for each of us: a new telescopic fishing rod and reel, all fitted out with line and leader and fly hooks and a creel, ready to go. Hazel was radiant and gave her father a hug. I was overwhelmed and enthusiastically shook Mr. Arthur's outstretched hand.

Mr. Arthur turned to me and said, "Let us, the three of us, go down next Sunday to Texas Creek, near Dickey's ranch, and try our luck there. I hear the creek is full of hungry trout."

So began a wonderful friendship between me, Fred Arthur, and his tomboy daughter Hazel. It was a most happy period of my life. Hazel and I had fallen in love and came to enjoy a lot of innocent hugging and kissing. Her father took us to several great fishing spots such as Yalakom Creek, Big Bar Creek, French Bar Creek, Duffy Lake, and Joffre Lake.

But my close relationship with Hazel and her family came to an abrupt ended in June 1939, just as Hazel and I were finishing Grade 9. I was twelve and Hazel was fifteen.

The Second World War had broken out, and my father found work at the ironworks in the wartime industrial boom town of New Westminster. My family followed my father and moved to New Westminster that July. I became a city boy, with the Carnegie New Westminster Public Library my centre of focus. No more Cayoosh and Texas Creek fishing trips with the Arthur family. Hazel and I did write to each other over several months, but she eventually found another boyfriend, and I, another girlfriend. The letters ceased. World War II went on in all its fury. I became a student at UBC in 1943, had to join the university's officer training corps, and forgot all about fishing in Lillooet's Cayoosh Creek for a good long while.

And while I often thought of Hazel and our Lillooet romance, when I was with my new girlfriend, Valentine Bouchard, I forgot all about Hazel.

By 1947, eight years later, I had finished high school, graduated from UBC, and graduated cum laude from the provincial Normal School in Vancouver. I began a career teaching high school mathematics, a career which lasted thirty-five years. As I knew from the beginning, I had been born to be a teacher.

I did return many times to Lillooet and took my four

children trout fishing in both Cayoosh Creek and Texas Creek
—but, unfortunately, I never again met up with Hazel or any
of the Arthur family.

Grade 8 school photo: Hazel, front row, third from the right,
with Gordon standing behind her.

Gordon's first class, Carleton school, Vancouver,
1951.

GORDON E. WHITNEY

Gordon, Gladstone highschool, Vancouver, 1983.

TWENTY-ONE
UNCLE ED WHITNEY

Uncle Ed Whitney arrived in Canada before World War I erupted in Europe in 1914. I never learned the exact year of his arrival. I think he was born in South Dakota in 1887, ten years before my father, Reuben, was born. In a family of eight children, Ed was the eldest. His parents were farmers, but family rumour was that the Whitney lineage stemmed from two ancestors, Eli Whitney, Jr. and his father, Eli Whitney, Sr., who in the early eighteenth century invented the cotton gin (or cotton engine) for extracting raw cotton from the seed, a giant step forward in the economy of the early American colonies.

The two Whitney men, senior and junior, also invented a musket that had replaceable parts. The American Revolutionaries used these muskets to successfully thwart the British naval blockade and henceforth to produce their own firearms. I really think my two ancestors invented mass production. I wonder what would be found if the present-day Whitney descendants had their DNA analyzed and compared it to Eli Whitney's DNA, because I think that Ed and Reuben Whitney inherited those same skills.

Uncle Ed was born with great mechanical skills. My father likewise was gifted as a carpenter, bricklayer, mechanic, and multi-tasker, but Ed gravitated toward manual skills such as watch repairing, at which he achieved great mastery.

My father was a family misfit who also left his home in South Dakota. I guess he was twenty-one at that time. He went west to Idaho, and, I think, worked on a farm owned by Harry and Effie Reynolds. He married my mother, Nina Reynolds, when she was fourteen. She bore her first child when she was fifteen. I often wondered how Reuben found his way to Lillooet. My mother said he was lured by letters from his older brother Ed.

I am only guessing at the route Uncle Ed took as he migrated to British Columbia from South Dakota, but I think he was lured by stories of the first Cariboo gold rush, which followed the earlier, defunct California gold rush in 1849. He was attracted by rumours that there was more placer gold to be extracted, farther north on the bars of the Fraser River.

However, I do know that my father went west to Idaho. He and Ed corresponded sporadically by letter, and Reuben was eventually lured to British Columbia by Ed's tales of placer gold being mined on the Fraser River bars around Lillooet.

Ed had fashioned a miniature hinged iron scoop and bolted it to the end of a twenty-foot steel pipe. The machine was operated manually by a thin wire cable running the length of the pipe and controlled by a notched trigger handle at its top end. Ed thought that if he lowered his invention into the Fraser River at a suitable location, he could scoop up gold-bearing gravel manually from the riverbed. Then the gravel could be washed by hand, with a gold pan, or with a more elaborate sluice box. I think the contraption was a total failure.

Ed Whitney was never on welfare. He made his living repairing watches: adjusting hair springs, replacing the jewelled bearings, and so on. I have no idea how he acquired the skill of watch repairing, but he was well-known in Lillooet as a man who could repair any watch. Ed was even remembered years later by a teacher who had started his career in Lillooet. "There was an Ed Whitney in Lillooet who repaired my watch for me during my first year of teaching. Any relation to you?"

"Yes," I said. "He was my uncle."

All the years Uncle Ed lived in Lillooet, he subscribed to the *Seattle Post-Intelligencer*—the *SPI*, he called it. Every Sunday in the summer, I was an uninvited guest, sitting on his front porch with his nodded permission, reading the voluminous *SPI* comic strips.

Uncle Ed sometimes let me observe him as he worked on a watch. I was fascinated by its complicated innards, especially when I could see the moving parts as Uncle Ed worked. A watch was classified by the number of jewels, red garnets or rubies, it possessed. Ed saved and catalogued all the spare parts that came from watches that had been abandoned, beyond all hope of repair. One time I saw him hold up, by its long chain, a pocket watch he had been working on. He swung it back and forth, finally letting it strike the wall once or twice. He explained to me that sometimes a watch he had worked on diligently without success was just being stubborn, and needed a good gentle thumping.

Ed Whitney eventually married a "half-breed" woman named Elvira Means—at least I thought they were married at the time. (In fact they were cohabiting.) I think Elvira was the daughter of an indigenous woman named Dottie and a Caucasian man, Dick Means, who farmed a small acreage on the Texas Creek road. There were two men in Lillooet named Means: Dave Means and Willard Means. I think they must have been Elvira's siblings.

I liked Willard. He always used to chat with me. He was born with a crippled left leg, and I felt sorry for him, but he was always cheerful when we talked. He used to ask me about school (and did I have a girlfriend?). He and his pal Harold Ostrander rebuilt an old Harley motorbike. One day, I came across Harold and Willard cleaning their machine. It was a beauty. I stood admiring it, and was thrilled when Harold told Willard to take me for a ride up and down the lane. Boy, oh boy. Sitting behind Willard with my arms around him and the wind blowing in my face, I was in heaven.

I was saddened three years later when I was told by one of my group of friends that Willard Means had committed suicide by lying in his bed with the muzzle of a 30:30 rifle under his chin. He pressed the trigger with his bare toe and blew his brains out. I ran off when someone began to describe how the blood and brains were splattered. I ran home, sat on the chopping block in our woodshed, and sobbed. No one heard me, and I wouldn't have cared if they had.

Years later, Tom Manson told me that Willard Means was really very depressed but put on a happy face when he was around people. Tom said Willard's crippled leg was the result of his mother being infected with venereal disease, maybe syphilis or gonorrhea. Tom went on to explain that Willard was probably overcome with loneliness because he couldn't attract a girlfriend. "I guess Willard couldn't see any point in going on. The suffering, the pain, was too much for him to handle. So he ended it. Poor bugger."

Elvira Means had come into Ed's life with a son, Wilbur, the product of a relationship between Elvira and a Chinese labourer. I can't remember being told the name of Wilbur's biological father, but I did learn that he worked on Mrs. Foster's farm, located on a fertile glacial bench just below town, similar to Tom Manson's property. I don't think Elvira and Ed were legally married, but her illegitimate son became known as Wilbur Whitney.

Wilbur, old enough to become an armoured car driver in the Italian campaign in World War II, survived without a scratch. Back home, in 1946, he became a skilled commercial truck driver and married one of the O'Donaghy girls, Eileen, a beautiful half-Irish, half-Siwash girl.

Eileen's father had come from Ireland, married an

indigenous Lillooet maiden, and sired seven handsome children: Eileen, Frida, Patrick, Jack, Martin, George, and Edith. Mr. O'Donaghy (shortened to Donaghy) was killed in an accident while working for the Department of Public Works. He fell off the back of a dump truck on the way from a slide area on the Seton Creek road, and his neck was broken. He died instantly.

Years later, I checked with Tom Manson on one of our return trips to Lillooet. "Tom, do you remember the Donaghys?"

"Sure," he replied. "I used to hire Jack and Martin to spray my orchard trees every spring."

"Do you remember any of the others?" I asked.

"Well," said Tom, "I remember when Wilbur Whitney went overseas in 1942. He came back in 1946 and died in Lillooet at age 52, of heart disease. He wasn't a Donaghy, but he married one. He left behind his widow Eileen and six sons, who still live in the Lillooet area."

"Do you remember any of the others? Frida, Edith, George?" I asked.

"No," said Tom. "I saw them a few times, I guess, on the Cayoosh flats, but I never talked with them, so I can't even remember what they looked like. If I met them today, I wouldn't know them. I did hear that Eileen, Wilbur Whitney's wife, was living in the Red Rock Manor."

I remembered the Donaghy clan, but I never met their mother. All four Donaghy boys, as I recall, were very tall, over six feet, and well proportioned. George, the youngest, was two years younger than me. He lived not far from me on the Cayoosh flats, with his mother.

One day, I made George a kite, which he loved, and gave him an old World War I army jacket that I had outgrown and half a bottle of cod-liver oil capsules. The Lillooet welfare doctor had given them to me because he said I looked anemic.

George Donaghy, raised on sockeye salmon, said the capsules were like candy.

George's mother, a skilled amateur seamstress, made the army jacket over to fit him and even found some brass buttons, which she sewed on. Believe me, George Donaghy was a handsome ten-year-old boy dressed in that jacket, flying the kite I had made for him.

Fifty years later, I met George at a reunion in Vancouver and he told me, during our long conversation, that I was his boyhood hero!

Elvira Means bore Ed Whitney four children: Henry, William, Walter, and Thelma. Thelma died, aged seven, from sugar diabetes. Henry was bright in school but socially backward, having neither mother nor father to give him guidance as a teenager. Ed was not an instructive father, and Elvira had deserted Ed after Thelma, the youngest, was born. Henry was an ill-mannered, bad-tempered teenager when I last saw him. He was sent to the Borstal home in New Westminster in at age sixteen for physically beating an indigenous teenage girl at a Saturday dance at the Indian reservation community hall. I can guess that Henry had made improper advances to the girl and, at her refusal, had attacked her. Henry himself was beaten to death in prison by a group of fellow inmates.

Probably because of Henry's violent death, Uncle Ed decided to return to the USA early in 1937. With my father's mechanical help, he rebuilt two of the eight old cars he had stored in his backyard. One car, a Ford, was given to Jim brothers' general store to settle a one-hundred-dollar grocery bill, and Ed used the second car, a Buick, to transport himself and his two remaining children, William and Walter, back to the USA, where he settled on Whidbey Island. William and Walter both grew up in Washington State and became skilled plumbers. I think they are still living on Whidbey Island.

In 1954, after I married Joanne and before we had children, I drove down with her one summer to Whidbey

Island. We drove in my tiny Morris Minor. It was about the size of a Baby Austin. That was quite a hazardous experience.

Uncle Ed was overjoyed at seeing us, and after we were up to date on family gossip, he showed us around his dwelling. When we entered the kitchen, we saw many heavy aluminum pots hanging on the kitchen wall—so many that I asked, "Uncle, why do you have so many pots, all alike? How can you use all of them?"

Uncle Ed answered, "Actually, I don't use but one set, but they were on sale so dammed cheap, I had to buy three sets. They were really cheap and of good quality. You never know when you'll need a new pot." He brought down a pot and passed it to Joanne. "Why don't you take a set home with you? You won't get that kind of quality up in Canada!" Joanne thanked him with a big smile and a hug. We had them for years. The wooden handles wore out long before the aluminum did.

Later, back home in Burnaby, I was showing my father the pots Ed had given us and suddenly remembered that when I was a child, I'd heard some Lillooet gossip about Ed. Rumour had it that he had crossed the US border with thousands of dollars' worth of gold and platinum dust hidden in secret compartments that he and my father had cleverly built into the chassis of the rebuilt Buick. My father had said absolutely nothing to us about it at the time, and at first I didn't believe the story. So, turning to my father in Burnaby, I asked, "Did Uncle Ed really smuggle a fortune in platinum into the USA?"

"Yes," my father answered. "You saw yourself how he got platinum out of black sand. Remember?"

"Do you mean when I used to watch Uncle Ed blow into a pile of black sand on a sheet of glass and, with tweezers, pick little grains of black and red stuff off the plate and put the pieces into bottles?"

"Yes, that's it!" said my father. "Those little grains were

platinum, small pieces of gold, and some small red garnets, commonly known as Fraser River rubies."

"So that's where the platinum came from?" I said.

"Yes," my father replied. "Uncle Ed used to buy black sand, magnetite, from struggling local miners, out-of-work fellows who worked the gold-bearing gravel bars around Lillooet in the low-water seasons of summer and autumn. The miners thought that your Uncle Ed Whitney was loony."

"But he wasn't, was he?" I said. "Was he the only one in Lillooet who knew how to get platinum out of black sand?"

"Yes," replied my father. "Ed was clever at a lot of things. He was the only one who knew how to do that."

"Old Uncle Ed," I said, "sure pulled the wool over their eyes, eh?"

Many years later, when I was an adult, my father told me a harrowing story about my Uncle Ed. Ed was always busy working at something during his waking hours, but one Saturday night, after he had put down his eyeglass and tweezers and gone to bed, he was awakened by a loud knock on his front door.

"Who in hell could that be?" Ed mumbled as he got out of bed. He grabbed the flashlight off his nightstand with his right hand and plucked his bathrobe off the chair with his left.

There came another, louder knock just as Ed made it to the door and opened it a crack to see who was knocking at such an hour. He shone the flashlight on his wristwatch. Eleven thirty.

He looked up. It was the police constable, Jim MacLaughlin. "Sorry to wake you up, Ed," he said, "but I've got a real tough medical problem up at the jail. I called in Dr. Ployart, but he couldn't solve it, and I called in old Doc Stewart. He came, but after taking one quick look at the problem, he said, "I can't handle this! Go, for Chrissake! Go and get Ed Whitney!"

"What is the problem?" asked Uncle Ed.

"Ed," said Jim, "I really can't tell you. You'll have to come and see for yourself."

"Okay," said Ed. "Just let me put on my pants, jacket, and shoes and get my watch repair kit."

Jim MacLaughlin replied, "Doc Stewart said to just bring your glass cutters!"

From the bedroom, Ed shouted, "Did you say *glass cutters*?"

"Yes," shouted Jim. "Doc Stewart told me you'd need glass cutters!" He added, "I'll be waiting outside in my car, so get a move on!"

In a few minutes, they pulled into the driveway of the police station. Ed was ushered into a cell, where an indigenous middle-aged woman lay groaning on a cot.

Ed looked into old Doc Stewart's eyes. Doc quickly said, "Ed, come and take look at this. I've never seen anything like it in my life." And he pointed to the moaning woman on the cot.

Ed said, "Well, what is so strange about a woman lying on a cot and moaning?"

Doc Stewart lifted up her dress above her waist. "Have a *good* look, Ed," he whispered.

"Oh, Jeezus help us," Ed declared. "Is that a wine bottle sticking out of her cunt?"

"Yes," said Doc. "Someone has shoved the wine bottle into her vagina, and it won't come out."

"You tried pulling it out?" asked Ed.

"Yes," Doc said. "I tried, and she screamed. So I tried squirting mineral oil around the neck of the bottle and even into her vagina, and she still screamed."

Ed scratched the bald spot in the centre of his scalp as he wondered what in hell he was supposed to do. He finally said, "Doc, do you think there's maybe a vacuum holding that bottle in there?" Doc nodded. "Well, if you men can gently put a piece of thin plywood under her hips and rear end to keep her steady, I think I can cut off the end of the bottle with my glass cutter." Then he whispered softly, "God, I hope she doesn't scream."

Moving as gently as they could, Doc Stewart and constable MacLaughlin gently slid the plywood under her. One lifted while the other slid the plywood into place. She moaned loudly, but she didn't scream.

Beads of sweat formed on Ed's brow as he carefully lifted the thick bottom end of the bottle and put a wad of soft cotton underneath, to cushion it while he cut. Then he poured turpentine on the middle of the bottle and rubbed it gently around the whole circumference, three inches up from its thick end to where the glass was at its thinnest. With his left hand supporting the upper part of the bottle, he quickly cut twice around the bottle with his glass cutter and tapped the end of the bottle with the handle. The bottle end fell off onto the cot.

Doc Stewart reached down and gently slid the wine bottle out of her vagina. "Go fetch a stretcher," said Doc, "so we can move her into a ground-floor room in the Victoria Hotel. And someone wake up Mrs. McNulty and ask her to sit and watch the patient until morning. I'll give the patient a sedative, so she'll get some rest."

"I hope I never see anything like that again as long as I live," said the constable in a weak voice. Turning to Uncle Ed, he said softly, "That was marvellous, Ed, really marvellous!"

And Doc Stewart, with a hand on Ed's shoulder and a huge grin on his face, chimed in with, "Ed, from now on, you'll have to add a phrase to the sign on your front door, so that it reads,
'E.E. Whitney
Watch Repairs and
Expert Glass Cutting.'"

TWENTY-TWO
THE SHAMAN

Six o'clock on a Sunday morning was a good time to try to catch a rainbow trout for dinner. So at five, I grabbed a piece of my mother's homemade bread off the table, smeared some Roger's golden syrup on it, drank a dipper of water from the pail in the corner by the stove, and went quietly out of the shack.

I took my fishing pole from where it hung on the wall, found a new fly hook in the packet in my shirt pocket, tied it to the leader, and headed for the fishing pool under the Cayoosh Creek Bridge.

It was a beautiful July morning. The air along the creek was fresh and cool. The sun had not yet risen over Fountain Ridge across the Fraser River. That was good, because it meant I would not cast my shadow on the water under the bridge. I hoped a big trout was lurking in the pool under there, and I didn't want to spook him. Trout are a very wary fish.

A month before, Tom Manson had remarked that every time I fished that part of Cayoosh Creek, I was walking on Indian reservation land. I had never heard that before. Well, I guess you learn something new every day when you're a kid.

I was almost at the bridge when my thoughts were

interrupted by a thudding coming from the bridge above me. My God, when I looked up, I could see under the brim of my baseball cap Old Kameans, the Lillooet Indian witch doctor, trotting as fast as he could along the roadway toward the bridge, glancing over his shoulder every two seconds. He was looking over his shoulder because someone about thirty feet behind him was throwing rocks at him—rocks twice the size of a baseball.

I was so scared I was frozen in my tracks.

I thought I recognized Dan Copeland as the rock thrower, but I wasn't sure. Anyway, when Old Kameans reached the bridge planking, the rock thrower saw me, stopped in his tracks, and turned abruptly around. He headed back along the roadway the way he had come.

I couldn't figure out what had gone on that morning, and after I caught two trout under the bridge, I just forgot about it. But three days later, when I went over to Tom Manson's place to reset my ling cod line, I ran into Tom as he worked on a hole in his barbed-wire fence. I told him what I had seen.

"Oh, yeah," said Tom. "That Saturday night, Dan Copeland held another home brew party in his house up the creek from you. He and his guests, including Old Kameans, got pissed to the gills. I guess they all passed out and slept, probably on the floor, until about five in the morning. The first two people up, Dan Copeland and Old Kameans, got into an argument over something. It made Old Kameans so furiously angry that he put an Indian curse on Dan Copeland.

"What is an Indian curse?" I asked.

"Don't ask me, I don't speak Siwash," said Tom. "But it must have been awful, because one of the guests heard Dan Copeland say he was going to kill Old Kameans, who bolted through the door and ran off, with Dan Copeland thirty feet behind him. They ran all the way across the big clay bluff, past the Tulip place, and out to the Cayoosh Creek road. You saw the tail end of the chase."

"Boy, I thought that one of those big rocks was going to hit Old Kameans on the back of his head and kill him for sure," I said.

"Well, he made it safely home," said Tom. "You probably saved his life, you know. But I don't think he'll show his face around town very soon."

"Why do they drink that home brew? I think they call it potato champagne," I said. "It must affect their brains."

"And," said Tom, "as Shorty Laidlaw told you, some of them don't know how to distill it without making fusil oil, and fusil oil has killed off some of them."

"Do you remember what happened to Melanie Copeland's mother?" I said.

"Yep, that was Dan Copeland's wife, Alice. She got drunk uptown one night, staggered down to the end of Conway's road, and tried to get across the railroad tracks onto the path down the Cayoosh Creek bluff. You know where Dan Copeland lives on Cayoosh Creek. Well, she didn't make it home. She fell down and passed out on the railroad tracks, right near the beginning of the path. Her head was resting on a rail, they figured, when the train ran over her. She was decapitated. It happened around 11:30, just as the PGE train was coming into Lillooet Station."

"God," I said. "What a way to die. But I guess being asleep, she didn't feel a thing. I don't remember her having a funeral."

"No," said Tom, "she didn't. Not in our cemetery, at least. She was buried in the Indian reservation graveyard up above Lillooet, near Scotchman's Flat. She had an Indian-Catholic funeral with a lot of wailing. Maybe you heard it but didn't know what it meant."

"I did hear some wailing from up on the reservation one time," I said. "My mother told me there was a funeral going for a baby and the women were wailing as they lowered the coffin in the ground. She said it was an old Lillooet Indian custom. I guess I could have asked Old Kameans about it, but I was afraid to."

"Yeah," said Tom, "he could have told you. He knows all about the history of Lillooet Siwash tribal customs."

I remembered, then, the time Roy Doherty dug the hole for a new telephone pole behind Joe Russell's yard and unearthed an Indian skeleton and relics, including some arrowheads. Teenage boys living nearby rushed to the scene with shovels and dug up the whole gravesite. They found deer bone needles, thousands of small seashells, polished elks' teeth with holes bored in them for making a necklace, argillite pipe bowls, serpentine grinding pestles, stone grinding bowls, and even a skull that was stained green from a decayed copper headband. You could see holes in the headband where someone must have stuck eagle feathers. Nobody told the boys to stop.

Old Kameans came a few days later, looked at the mess, and shook his head in disbelief. He was very upset.

"And he had every right to be," Tom said of that sad affair. "What would we say if someone came along and dug up some of the old graves in our cemetery? Someone should have phoned Victoria and had an expert from the provincial museum come up and examine the site."

The site turned out to be just what everyone in town suspected: an ancient Indian cemetery. Old Kameans must have been shocked when he saw the desecration.

I was looking at the disturbed graves one morning—a real mess—when Old Kameans happened by. I started putting bones back into the holes, using a stick.

Old Kameans turned to me and said, "You are a good boy. Those are the bones of my peoples."

Lilooet 1894 (or 1864?) Gov't Reps w/ Lillooet Indians

Lillooet Indians and government agents, late 1800s.

Ode to an Indian Chief

O Chief,
Your bones lie bare in shawls of sand
Bereft of feathers fine sprung
From copper discs now green in age
Your arms unbanded, legs unsheathed
From shells quills sun-shattered beads
Buckskin and a hundred scattered
ornaments

Your ribs lyre in a willow wind
Your once beat heart chokecherry seed
In sand your bones unarrowed now
Spew out love wind tossed away
For that once beauty maid
Who honed the blade of your
Desire

Your two ghosts peer
From those blind socket eyes
Her lips moan with yours as willows weep over
Your two voices rustle summer maize as
Two stalks rusk together in a hot wind and
Gaunt carpal bones that clutch an argillite pipe
Once held a flesh hard hand against a lover's
Thigh

O Chief,
Your smile glints from sagebrushed sand
Your skull grinning thunder in a clay sun
For secrets lie within your ochred bones
Your flesh has stirred that earth awhile
And now when horse-worn trails mound your grave
You thrust through wounds wisely
Flowers out of
Dust

Death of a Small Child

The Indian village greets the rising sun
voices wailing through aspen trees under a blue sky.
below, Lillooet townspeople waken and listen sadly
compassion echoing off grey roofs up into white trees.

Indian men women children stand and wail
keening loudly under a Cariboo mourning sky
eyes sad and hollowed out by tears for one child
taken away too sudden into death's easy hands.

"Do they wail to appease the Spirits' returning?"

"No, the Land of Death holds tribal mysteries,
telling us how to grieve over the death of a small child
so innocent and so young."

Mount Brew bends its late-afternoon shadows
embracing fear to ease the longing for love
and the drying of tears and accepting of pain
caressing the moccasined buckskin-trodden ground

Weary dogs lie comatose in cool shade
Lill'a'wa't women tend their cooking fires
tear-streaked faces cooled by a Cayoosh breeze
blowing softly over sweet-smelling sage.

"Why, Shaman, do Lill'a'wa't people wail to an empty sky?"

"Why, O White Priest, do Lillooet people wail in a wooden church?
We Lill'a'wa't people talk to God straight up in a real sky. He hears us!
Can God hear you pray to Him under your church's heavy wooden sky?"

TWENTY-THREE
LIFE ON THE CAYOOSH CREEK FLATS

It was after dinner, around six, when the three Miller kids
criss-crossed the flat to where my brother Doug and I
straddled a driftwood log that we had dragged up from the
creek last summer. It had been a gargantuan task but a labour
of love. We loved that log and were inordinately proud of it.
Who else could boast such a bizarre piece of patio furniture,
right in their yard? It was too hot to sit on the log during
summer days, but this June evening, the air had begun to cool,
with the sun sinking over the ridge behind the town.

Doug and I had been leaning back, looking up into the sky,
and admiring the kite I had made for him three days earlier. He
had launched it and tethered it to a young cottonwood tree
about one hundred feet from our shack, and it was still up
there, blown to and fro by the powerful breeze that came off
the creek day in and day out, all year long.

The breeze that powered our kites was a godsend to all of
us on the flats because it made our Cayoosh flats mosquito
proof. Mosquitos need still air in which to launch and fly
around. It's how they sense the air currents and detect their
warm-blooded victims. We Cayoosh Creek residents were
lucky. We could sleep outside at night and look up at the stars

235

and the Milky Way, whereas residents in the town one
hundred feet above had to sleep in hot summer bedrooms or
under mosquito netting. And, too, one had to put up with the
night noises of people, motor cars, and drunks—arguing,
swearing, and passing up and down Main Street into the early
hours of the morning. On the Cayoosh flat, we had to contend
only with the noise from Cayoosh Creek as it flowed by on its
way to the Fraser River.

The noise of three pairs of running shoes crunching on
gravel drew Doug and me away from kite watching and back
to the imminent arrival of the Miller kids. We glanced, now
and then, as they closed the gate in the front yard of their
neat log cabin and walked the one hundred yards of barren
clay and gravel flat toward our poverty-stricken, tarpaper
shack.

The Miller kids came daily after supper to visit. And the
visit always included a request to play a game of hide-and-
seek: "Let's play hide-and-seek. C'mon, let's! Not it, not it, not
it," they chorused.

It always ended with me being "it." I didn't mind. They
were nice kids, so friendly. Despite our age differences, Doug
and I both felt a strong bond of friendship with them. Mabel
was almost twelve, four years older than Doug; Mary was ten;
and Albert was eight. I was senior at thirteen.

Doug and I envied the Miller kids their nice log house and
yard with its flowers and vegetables. Their strip of arable land
was located at the bottom of the pine-treed slope from the town
flat above and sat about one hundred yards back from the
creek. The Millers were another lower-class family, some of
them descendants of poor ranchers, some of them white men
who had "married" indigenous brides, but their log house sat
on dirt beneath a cliff, which sheltered them from the cold
north wind that blew down the Fraser in winter. And an
aquifer flowing out of a sandy layer at the bottom of the cliff
provided fresh cold water from the glacier on Mount McLean.

(It provided water for a string of small holdings on the same impervious clay strata.)

Our shack, perched on the edge of Cayoosh Creek only one hundred feet back from the bank, was completely exposed to view. We were unprotected from the north wind, which engulfed us in winter. "It's cold enough," Old Man Thompson used to say, "to freeze the balls off a brass monkey." We had only gravel, sand, and rounded river boulders on which to put our feet. Our front yard was completely lacking in soil. This was due to the annual flooding of the Fraser, twelve feet at times, which backed up the Cayoosh as well and had flushed, over the centuries, all the topsoil down into the Fraser River Delta at Vancouver.

So the Millers had soil, we had stones. They had running water, we had to carry our water one hundred feet from Cayoosh Creek in buckets. But we were lucky: at least it wasn't two hundred feet! I didn't really mind, because the creek was my second home. I was an avid trout fisherman, probably the best rainbow trout fisher among my peers.

It was an easy five-minute walk for the Miller kids to reach our front door, so they were handy playmates. Beggars can't be choosers, after all. But that's not fair. They were nice kids. And maybe I was attracted to Mabel. She was cute, a few inches shorter than me, blue-eyed like her mother. Mabel had light-brown hair and a slim figure just beginning to show a few bumps and curves. But Mabel was not socially acceptable to me as a possible girlfriend because despite our closeness in age, she was in Grade 6 and I was in Grade 9. I had been skipped three grades in school, and I would be subjected to daily ridicule from my Grade 9 peers if they ever found out.

On the other hand, how could they find out? Mabel was in Grade 6. Her classroom and its play area were way off in the northern half of the school grounds. We never ran into each other during school hours.

So therein lay my social dilemma. If I ever wanted to see

my Grade 9 schoolmates after school, I had to walk back up
into town, a mile away above our flats. The Miller kids were
physically available after school hours and remote from social
contact with any of my other friends.

Anyway, none of my schoolmates were my companions
even during the day. I was three years younger and three
inches shorter than them. From the beginning, I was socially
handicapped by starting school prematurely, by being a
physical runt, and later, by being sexually immature. I was
academically competent but subject to physical torment by my
classmates. The last such horrible episode had occurred when I
was eight, on my first day in Grade 5. I came home that day
with a dirty shoe print on one cheek. David Dillon, age twelve,
had tripped me on my way home, knocked me off my feet, and
stood with one foot on my face. I told my mother, who told my
father, and he went next door to the Dillon house and, in front
of Mrs. Dillon, threatened David with mayhem if he ever
touched me again.

By the time I got into Grade 9, my last year in Lillooet,
most of my male classmates had gone through puberty, volubly
so, and the annual class photographs show me a good head
shorter than everyone else. My female classmates had already
begun to wear brassieres. I admit I was attracted to those girls,
but they never acknowledged my attempts to be noticed. My
one asset, in the eyes of most of my classmates, was my
scholastic ability, which didn't attract attention of the romantic
sort in this Lillooet milieu. None of the girls in Grade 9 would
have been seen dead with me as a boyfriend. I was doomed to
remain a child bachelor, doomed to disassociate myself from
girls my own age because they populated only the lower
grades. Socially, I was a lower-class-upper-class snob!

So I accepted this situation and continued to enjoy the
after-school company of the three Miller kids. I sensed that
Mabel wanted me to be her boyfriend. She was nice to look at,
and she was definitely pubescent.

I sound as though I had expertise in sizing up female bodies, which was not the case. But I occasionally peeked at Mabel's chest, which was hidden, but not opaquely so, under her loose-fitting cotton blouse. I could detect—or at least I thought I could detect—the presence of burgeoning flesh. I wanted to think, "burgeoning tits," but shame overcame me, and I stuck, even in my thoughts, to the term *flesh*. But I could, at least, see nipples as they pushed their points against the fabric of her blouse.

On a warm Sunday evening, the last day in June, the five of us were once more playing hide-and-seek. Again I was forced to be "it," but I enjoyed seeing the enthusiasm they exhibited so gleefully, for this simple game. The glee was contagious. And it was relaxing to forget all the tension generated by being the runt in my Grade 9 class.

I was calm as I crept as quietly as I could on the gravel, trying to spot a hider so I could race back to the corner of our shack and shout "one, two, three" before the others could get there and shout "home free!"

I had only crept a short distance when I found Mabel crouched behind a nearby bush, obviously wanting to be caught by me. Wow. She looked so inviting that I blew my cool, bent down, and put my mouth on hers. I kissed her, right on the lips. It was nice, a little out of control, and I slipped my hands inside the wide-open neck of her blouse and fondled her immature, short, smooth, and pendulous cucumber breasts. I was shocked by their shape. I had thought that girls' breasts were shaped differently, more like oranges cut in half.

Now, in my advanced years, I wonder why I didn't check out the lower part of her body. I could have said that I was just "playing doctor," and she could be my patient. But I was never quick-witted in an emergency.

This all happened on Sunday night. On Monday, when I arrived at my classroom, ready to write the final government exams, I was told by my teacher to go home. He said I'd been

promoted to Grade 10 and didn't have to write any exams. So I
went out into the empty senior playground area and sat on a
bench in the bleachers, sad and lonely. I would have preferred
to be writing the exams with my classmates. At least I would
have been near those big girls with their curvy hips, ample
bosoms, and—oh, yes—pretty faces.

Guess who appeared before me where I sat on the bench,
still moping? It was Mabel Miller, the girl I had kissed on the
mouth and whose breasts I had fondled the previous evening.
She stood in front of me, smiling, not saying a word, but there
was a look on her face that troubled me. She wanted me, I
could tell. And I knew what was going through her mind. She
thought that my actions last night were proof positive that I
wanted her too. God, I was scared to death. Maybe she
thought I was going to marry her someday.

So I hightailed it out of there and avoided Mabel for the
rest of the week, never once sitting on our beautiful driftwood
log outside our shack. But her enthusiasm didn't dim, as I was
to find out two months later when I was in Grade 10 at the
Duke of Connaught High School in New Westminster.

At the end of that week in Lillooet, our last week in town,
my mother packed up all our personal belongings in some old
suitcases. Tom Manson, my Cayoosh Creek mentor, cranked
up his old Model T Ford and drove us with our luggage up
Station Hill to the PGE Railway (now BC Rail) station, where
we caught the eight o'clock passenger train to Squamish. At
Squamish, we boarded the Union Steamship, and three hours
later we were in Vancouver Harbour.

Dad had found work at the Alaska Pine sawmill in the
Lower Mainland and had sent for us. He was there to meet us
at the harbour, and a taxicab took us to 618 Agnes Street in the
slums of New Westminster. That was my home for eight years,
until I graduated from UBC.

As I had suspected, I got a letter that August from Mabel.
How did she ever get my address? It was a very affectionate,

drippy letter, but it gave me the news about what had happened to our shack and who the new occupants were. We had left everything we owned except our personal belongings. So someone got a fully-equipped shack, free for the taking.

I burned Mabel's letter in the kitchen stove. She wanted me to write to her. To hell with that! Oh, I thought about Mabel a few times in the weeks that followed, but what I thought about more, and missed terribly, was the beautiful driftwood log Doug and I used to sit on after supper. I wondered what would happen to it. Maybe the new owners of our shack had already sawn it into stove lengths and cut it up for firewood, the bastards!

Grade 9 class, 1939: Gordon is 2nd row, far right (he was three years younger than his classmates).

GORDON E. WHITNEY

LILLOOET HIGH SCHOOL
QUARTERLY REPORT

Grade *Nine*

Pupil's Name *Gordon Whitney*

SUBJECT	PUPIL'S MARK	MEDIAN
Algebra	62	58
Arithmetic	70	59
Art		
Chemistry *Spelling*	94	86
Composition	80	66
French Authors	95	84
French Grammar	76	62
General Science	78	58
Geography		
Geometry	63 71	74
Grammar		
Health and Physical Education	83	78
Latin Authors		
Latin Grammar		
Literature	96	70
Music		
Physics		
Social Studies	82	66

Total 881   Average 80.09   Rank of Pupil 1

REMARKS:

Gordon's Grade Nine report card: Gordon was ranked #1
student every year.

242

The shack built by Gordon's dad on the boulder flats of
Cayoosh Creek.

TWENTY-FOUR
MY FRIEND SHORTY

It was the last Monday in June, the same day that I had been excused from writing my Grade 9 government exams. I was homeward bound on the dirt road at the bottom of Station Hill. I was about to make a right turn and walk across the flats to our shack when I noticed Shorty Laidlaw striding across the Cayoosh Creek Bridge. He waved and waved again, and I waved back. Shorty was one of my mentors.

He yelled something, but I couldn't make it out. He was too far away, and the Cayoosh breeze blew his words downwind toward the Fraser River. So I waited until he caught up with me.

"How come you're not in school?" he asked. His face was so close to mine I could smell onion and bacon on his breath. He'd probably just eaten breakfast, and it was already ten thirty.

"Mr. Kramer, the principal and my Grade 9 teacher, kicked me out," I replied. "He said he'd promoted me to Grade 10 and I didn't have to write the Grade 9 government exams. But all the rest of my class had to write. So I'm alone. Jeezus crappo mundo!"

"You lucky young bugger," said Shorty. "Why are you so downhearted? You should be as happy as a clam."

"Well, what's so happy about it? It's lonely out of school when you're the only one. There's no one to talk to, no one to have fun with, no Grade 9 girls to look at, nothing to do but sit on my ass on a bench in the empty grandstand. And, to top it all off, some silly Grade 6 girl came over and wanted to start a conversation with me. So I left."

Shorty smiled and nodded. "Who was the girl? Anyone I know?"

"Never mind." I scowled at Shorty. "Let's drop the subject!"

"Okay, okay," Shorty said, laughing at my discomfort. "Why don't you come with me? I'm going over to Tom Manson's. I have to check my set line in the lagoon. I set a line every night after supper."

"Jeezus, Shorty," I almost shouted in amazement. "I didn't know you knew how to fish. I thought you didn't even like fishing!"

"I *didn't* know a bloody thing about fishing. I *didn't* like fishing. But now I like it." Another big grin creased Shorty's round face. "But you never know about life, do you? Tom Manson taught me how to fish and even loaned me all the equipment. So bloody simple, after all my years of knowing bugger-all about fishing, and Tom rigged me out for free. All I needed was some heavy salmon line, a couple of big number-seven hooks, and a six-inch PGE railroad spike. And haven't I been lucky? Every morning this last week, I've caught a big freshwater ling cod right there in Tom's lagoon. And they are delicious fried in bacon fat, almost as tasty as trout."

Shorty was out of breath. I'd never before heard him string together so many words in one sentence. He was really hepped up. Of course, he loved food. He was addicted to food. And he was quite chubby: mute evidence of a good appetite.

"Tom has a helluva lot of equipment hanging on the wall of

his back porch," Shorty continued. "I bet he'd lend you some so you could start fishin' for ling like I do. It's somethin' to do, somethin' to make you forget all about school. Somethin' to make you forget about that Grade 6 girl."

Why did Shorty have to go on about that girl? I was embarrassed, and I wondered who else knew about Mabel. I felt myself blushing, and when Shorty's grin widened, I said, "Come on. Let's go see Tom Manson about fitting me out with some fishing tackle."

We strolled along the dirt road toward Tom Manson's gate, and we passed a small shack on the left, nestled up against the Station Hill road. I drew Shorty's attention to it and to the many flowerpots hanging from the branches of the two cottonwood trees. The pots were wrapped in newspaper and tied with twine. That was weird. And I couldn't see any flowers in the pots. I asked Shorty about it.

"There are begonia flowers hidden in those pots," Shorty said. "They're a delicate kinda flower. They've gotta be protected from direct sunlight, so Charlie protects them with newspapers, keeps them from the direct sun. Otherwise they'd dry up and keel over in the heat. Didn't you know that's Old Charlie Mitchell's place? I guess you never met him. Begonias is his hobby. He's an expert on those kinda plants. He knows one helluva lot about plants, and he makes great elderberry wine, too. I had some last Christmas at his open house. Charlie is a man of many talents."

"Open house?" I asked. "What's an open house, Shorty?"

"Well," said Shorty, "It means your *house* is *open* to visitors. And Charlie Mitchell, every Christmas, invites his friends in to drink some of his homemade wine, eat some food, get a little drunk, forget their troubles, tell a few jokes, and have a good time. Some people bring in a case of beer or a bottle of hard liquor. You wouldn't know what that is. I bring a bottle of Dan Copeland's home brew. That's powerful stuff, made out of dandelion flowers. Dan Copeland and I have a deal. I trade him ling cod for home brew from time to time. But don't *you* ever touch that kind of liquor."

We went through Tom Manson's gate, being very careful to latch the gate properly after us. There were lots of wild horses and loose cows wandering around. In five minutes, we were knocking on Tom's back door, and a half hour later we were headed to the lagoon, carrying thirty feet of salmon twine, two large hooks, a six-inch-long PGE railroad spike, and a big can of earthworms we had dug up in Tom's vegetable garden.

On the way to the lagoon, Shorty took over. He was puffed up about his teaching skills. He knew his stuff. I could tell from my own experience as a trout fisherman — or fisher boy, at my age. I guessed Shorty was about fifty, but he could have been older.

Soon, under Shorty's tutelage, I had tied the railway spike to one end of the salmon twine, made two loops in the twine about ten inches up from the spike, fastened the two hooks onto the loops, and put three fat earthworms on each hook. I tied the free end of the twine to the trunk of a nearby cottonwood tree, about fifteen feet back from the water. Then I walked down to the edge of the water and picked up the baited end of the line, which I twirled around my head three times and tossed out into the lagoon. Thanks to the railroad spike, the line immediately sank out of sight in the murky water of the Fraser River.

Shorty nodded his approval. "Leave it there all night, and tomorrow morning you'll have one or two big lings to take home."

"Wow," I said. "That's an easy way to catch fish. What time in the morning should I come back?"

"Meet me here at nine o'clock," said Shorty. "Is that okay?"

"Yeah, sure, I'll be here," I said as we parted.

Shorty headed for town, and I headed for our shack across the Cayoosh flats. You can guess I was really excited. Two ling cod to take to my mother for dinner tomorrow!

"Yahoo!" I shouted as I walked away.

Shorty smiled after me, waved, and shouted, "See you tomorrow morning."

Next morning, when I arrived at the lagoon at nine o'clock, Shorty wasn't there. So I pulled in my line and found that I had hooked two ling cod, two feet long each. I unhooked the fish. They were dead, so I didn't have to knock them on the head with a stick. I rebaited my hooks from the can of worms left over from the day before, then I tossed the line and sinker back into the water.

I squatted down on the sand, gutted both fish with my red-handled jackknife, buried the guts in the sand, rinsed out the insides of the fish down at the water's edge, wiped off my knife blade with a big cottonwood leaf, dried it on my pant leg, and shoved it back into my hip pocket. Then, careful not to get any fish slime on my pant leg, I carefully coiled the two fish, head to tail, into my home-made creel.

As I shouldered my creel, I thought about waiting around for Shorty to arrive, but I decided instead to knock on Tom Manson's door on my way back to the main gate, to thank him again for lending me the fishing gear. Just as I got to the front gate, Tom hailed me from the doorway of the shed on the opposite side of the widened path that served as a roadway. The shed was where Tom stored his tree-spraying equipment.

Every spring, when the apple trees first blossomed, Tom hired the two O'Donaghy boys, Jack and Martin, to spray them to prevent the coddling moths from laying eggs inside their flowers. Otherwise, baby apples would form around the eggs and trigger them into hatching into caterpillars. As the fruit ripened and became full of sugar, the caterpillars, or tiny "worms," proceeded to eat and grow fat, tunnelling their way right through the apples and leaving brownish wormholes behind them. Finally, they would crawl out of the apple, fasten themselves with silk to the underside of a leaf or branch, and morph into chrysalids. Inside these, they morphed into adults

and emerged into the world as quite pretty adult moths, a real
natural miracle!

Some people wouldn't eat a wormy apple with its brownish
worm tunnels, but I did. I just ate my way around the
wormholes and tossed them away with the core and the stem. I
figured that after watching an apple tree produce beautiful
flowers, tiny apples, and fully-grown fruit with pink cheeks
and that sweet apple smell, I'd be a damn fool to toss away
such a miracle because of a few wormholes! So I ate lots of
wormy apples when I was a boy. Nowadays, unless you grow
your own apple tree, you can't find an apple with a wormhole
in it. Buy as many apples as you want—you won't find one
wormy apple because of the wide use of pesticides and the
close inspection of fruit before it is placed on the produce
stands. "Is that a good thing or bad thing?" I ask myself. I'm
not sure I have an answer.

"Did you get any fish?" Tom asked.

"Yeah, I got two beauties," I replied, patting my creel. "I
thought Shorty would be here, but he didn't show."

"Oh, he was here, all right, about two hours ago," Tom
said. "He got his fish and left, saying he had an offer for some
wood cutting at Dickey's farm down Texas Creek way. They
were going to pick him up with their truck at a quarter to eight
at the south fork off the Seton Lake road. He told me to tell
you he was sorry, but he had to go early, and he hoped to see
you real soon."

After I had pondered Shorty's message, Tom went on,
"Have you got a few minutes? I'd like to take you in to meet
my mother. I've told her a few things about you, and she'd like
to meet you. You can hang your creel on the nail in the wall by
the back door. Your fish will be safe there."

Tom opened the kitchen door and led me into the kitchen,
where his mother was seated at the table reading the *Bridge
River Lillooet News*, the local newspaper. She smiled as she
turned to face us, taking off her reading glasses and putting

them gently on the table. She was pretty. She had a real friendly face, a happy face.

"Mother," Tom said, "I'd like you to meet a young friend of mine, Gordy—I mean Gordon—Whitney."

She smiled again and beckoned me to an empty chair across from her. Tom sat down in the empty chair beside mine, so I quickly said, "I'm very glad to meet you, ma'am," and sat down.

"Tom has told me many times," Mrs. Manson said, "that you are a bright student, only turned thirteen at Christmas and just completed Grade 9." I must have blushed a bit. "And," she went on, "he tells me you are a great trout fisherman."

Tom could see that I was becoming embarrassed, so he broke in with, "Yes, Mother, he is that, and last night he just caught two nice ling cod. First time he's fished for ling." Then, "Oh, gosh, I forgot that Gordy's fish are hanging in his creel on the wall outside. We'd better let him go on his way so he can get home and put the fish in cold water. Otherwise they'll go bad before his mother can cook them for supper."

Mrs. Manson nodded in agreement. "Yes, he should." To me, she said, "It was kind of you to drop in to say hello, Gordon." She smiled at me again. "Tom, you must bring young Mr. Whitney back again so he can stay longer and we can give him a cup of tea and some of my cookies."

"I will do so, Mother," said Tom over his shoulder as we passed through the kitchen door and I retrieved my fish off the wall.

"How about meeting me at the bottom of Station Hill this afternoon, Gordy?" Tom said. "At one o'clock, if you're free? I have to go to the post office for our mail, and you and I can talk on the way up the hill."

"I'm free for sure," I said. "I've got lots of time now. I'll be there at one."

As I trotted across the Cayoosh flat toward our shack, I was overcome with joy. "Wow!" I mumbled to myself. "She called me 'young Mr. Whitney.' Nobody ever called me that before!"

At one o'clock, as Tom and I started up Station Hill and rounded the first bend in the road fifty yards ahead, I could see a man sitting on a block of concrete, his head down, a shovel handle leaning on one shoulder. He was sitting right next to the ditch under his feet. The ditch, of course, was located on the sloping inner side of the road.

I was just about to ask Tom if he knew who it was, but Tom had placed his right index finger on his lips and put his left hand on my shoulder. "Shh," he whispered. "You'll wake him up. Let's try to sneak up on him." So we continued stalking as quietly as we could, barely breathing and gradually shortening the distance between us and the sleeping figure. Finally we were within ten feet.

Tom whispered, "It's Jim Folkes. Don't make a sound." As we crept closer, I could recognize the figure. It was the father of George, Herby, and Edith Folkes, kids who went to Lillooet Elementary School.

"Let's turn and look away from him, down at the river," Tom whispered. "I'll make a sudden loud noise to wake him up. If we turn around fast, we'll see him jump into action."

Tom coughed really loud, and we looked around just in time to see Mr. Folkes snap awake, frantically pick up his shovel, and start madly digging, deepening and widening the ditch.

Tom laughed and said, "Gee, Mr. Folkes, we're sorry. We didn't notice you there. We were so busy looking at the scenery."

Mr. Folkes only nodded, his head down as he kept on digging.

As we walked on up the hill, Tom explained, "This little project is for the older guys on the dole. They have to put in so many hours of work to qualify for the small amount of welfare they get from the government each month. This ditch is important, in a way, because it drains excess water from the two-hundred-gallon steel water tank we just passed. The ditch the old man is working on lets the water drain so it won't overflow and erode the roadway. The ditch drains into a gravel pit at the bottom of Station Hill. Maybe you've noticed it."

"Yes, I have," I said, "but it drains into a pond just off the road and breeds a lot of mosquitos and frogs. I can hear them chirping at night. They make almost as much noise as the crickets do."

"Well," said Tom, "the frogs are important because they live on mosquitoes and their larvae. You don't notice the mosquitoes at night, like we do, because the Cayoosh breeze keeps them away from your shack. But I have to place screens on all my windows, and I have to make sure the screen doors are shut tight, even during the day."

"Tom," I asked as we walked on, "is Shorty on welfare? And doesn't he have to work, digging the ditch like Mr. Folkes? All the time I've lived on the flats and walked back and forth to school, I've never ever seen Shorty working on the ditch."

"And you never will," replied Tom. "Shorty *is* on welfare, but he's found a way out of doing pick-and-shovel work, especially in public. Shorty is a proud man."

"How did he manage that?" I asked.

"Well," said Tom, "you know old Doc Stewart? He's a pal of Shorty's. Now, don't you ever repeat this, because it could get Shorty into trouble. Maybe Doc Stewart, too."

"Gee," I said, "Shorty is a good friend of mine. I would never say anything to get him in trouble."

"Well, here is how Shorty gets out of ditch digging. When he gets the call to do some work on Station Hill every so often, he follows Doc Stewart's advice. The day before he is to report for work, after he gets the notice to gather up his pick and shovel at the government works office, he gets up, doesn't eat any breakfast, puts a wad of chewing tobacco in his mouth, and leaves it there in his cheek while he runs up Station Hill to Doc Stewart's back door. Doc immediately examines Shorty with his stethoscope, notes Shorty's very rapid heartbeat—caused, of course, by the overdose of nicotine—and writes Shorty a certificate stating that he is unfit for hard labour because of a heart condition and fit for office work only."

I laughed so hard I doubled over, and when I finally recovered my composure, I said, "Can you imagine Shorty working in the government office?"

"God, no!" Tom chuckled. "He probably can barely read and write. Just remember, now. You promised never to repeat this to anyone, and especially never to let Shorty know that you know."

"Don't worry, Tom." I grinned. "My lips are sealed!"

Half an hour later, after we had passed the cemetery, Tom remarked, "Shorty occasionally makes five dollars for digging a grave."

Tom and I had reached Main, and we were sitting on the elaborate green bench in front of Gordon Santini's pool room, watching the world go by.

"Where do you think Shorty's from?" I asked Tom. "He talks with an English accent, a tiny bit like Doc Stewart but not as refined."

"Shorty comes from Liverpool. That's in England, on the seacoast—the Atlantic Ocean, I think. Gordon Santini says that Shorty comes from the slums. He says Shorty speaks with a strong Scouse accent when he gets angry."

"How old do you think Shorty is?" I asked.

"Nobody seems to know exactly," Tom continued. "Maybe he's fifty-five or even sixty. But he is strongly built. He may be only five-foot-two, but look at his arms! He's small but powerful, maybe from digging graves."

Tom got up to pick up his mail at the post office, and he left me sitting there, thinking about Shorty. Yes, Shorty was small, but he had hairy, muscular arms, a thick, hairy chest, and

strong legs. I never noticed his teeth, but he always had a
ready smile on his face. People liked and trusted him. Shorty
was always ready to do odd jobs, jobs most people didn't want
to do themselves, like digging a hole for a new outdoor toilet.
He was a hard worker, and his rates were very reasonable. I
wondered how Shorty came to live in Lillooet. England was a
long way off. From what I later heard, Shorty signed on to a
freighter in Liverpool in the summer of 1932, working as a
deckhand, and a month later, when the ship docked in
Vancouver, he got his wages and jumped ship. He asked
around at the right places and soon located the Hobo Jungle
near the waterfront. He was a good listener.

He heard some good things about a town in the Cariboo
called Lillooet and made up his mind to ride the rods on a PGE
freight train headed for Prince George. He and a dozen other
hobos hopped off the train that night in Lillooet, at ten thirty.
One of them had been to Lillooet before and advised them to
sneak off over the cliff from the freight yards, down to the
Cayoosh Creek flats below.

Shorty later told me that his fellow hobos had described
Lillooet as a nice, friendly little town. So over the next few
days, while hanging around on the Cayoosh flats, he surveyed
the prospects for survival in our town and decided to stay.
Shorty liked what he saw, and in the months that followed, he
met quite a few friendly people, made some spare-time job
contacts, and settled into a survival routine that had a future.
He even became Lillooet's permanent gravedigger. Lillooet had
acquired a new citizen.

Shorty was a survivor, a clever scrounger. Everything in his
cramped, eight-by-twelve, sod-roofed cabin was either
scrounged, borrowed, stolen, or handmade for him by a friend.
His stove, for example, was made from an abandoned twenty-
five-gallon oil drum. He had talked Jim Larter, the blacksmith,
into converting the oil drum into a crude all-purpose stove,
which he used to heat his cabin and cook his Spartan meals. It

was a neat object, complete with a flatiron, sheet-metal lid on its top and a hinged cast-iron door on one side. It was ideal for inserting chunks of driftwood, which Shorty salvaged from the Fraser riverbank in the dry summer after the river had retreated to well below the high-water mark.

Shorty did odd jobs for Jim Larter to pay for the favours Mr. Larter did for him in return. Someone else—probably Karl Lorenz, the town carpenter—had given Shorty an old handsaw and a hatchet, which he used to saw the driftwood into stove lengths.

And a fellow hobo had shown Shorty how to make a stovepipe out of empty Pacific condensed milk cans. He used a hand can opener to first cut out both ends of a can. Then, with tinsnips borrowed from the smithy when Jim Larter wasn't looking, he cut strips in one end and crimped it, making it smaller so it could be fitted into another can, end on end, until the pipe was long enough to go through a hole in the sod roof (and high enough above the roof so as to not start a fire). Thus Shorty, with his limited skills, had rendered the cabin fireproof.

"Look at that," chortled Shorty, looking at the long milk-can stovepipe. "Bloody mass production, that's what it is, bloody mass production!"

On one occasion, I was invited into the cabin. "How can you live in such a cramped space?" I asked him.

"It's perfect," he said, and he pointed to the bunk fastened onto the wall near the stove. "When I lie on my bed, I can not only see everything I own, but I can reach out and touch it as well. And in winter, when the cold north wind blows down the Fraser Canyon," he went on, "I'm as warm as toast, as snug as a bug in a rug, as long as I bank the fire in the stove to last until daybreak. And," he added, "there's room for two people."

I didn't get the significance of that remark until later on. I didn't think Shorty had the charm to attract women. But, in fact, Shorty used the cabin as a love nest. I heard from Tom

Manson that Shorty never ran out of indigenous female mates. My guess is that he plied them with Dan Copeland's home brew. That could have been Shorty's aphrodisiac. I hoped that he never sired any illegitimate children from these liaisons. Maybe he did, but no one in Lillooet ever accused him of it.

I left Lillooet in 1939. I heard, in 1970, that Shorty had died at age eighty in the Lytton Hospital. Later I searched the Lillooet cemetery records, but Shorty was not even mentioned. Tom Manson told me he wasn't buried in Lillooet, where he had dug so many graves for others. I guess he should have dug a spare one for himself.

Rest in peace, Shorty!

TWENTY-FIVE

DOUGHNUTS

By 1939, my family and I had left Lillooet for good. Although we settled in the slums of New Westminster, by some stroke of ill fortune, I was one of the only poor students at the local high school I attended. Surrounded by a bunch of rich kids, who were a few years older than me to boot, I found myself growing nostalgic for the freedom and open spaces of the Cayoosh Creek flats and wondering how our old friends were getting on in Lillooet.

Years later, friends I'd stayed in touch with told me stories about Lillooet in wartime. One such story was related to me by a man named Bill Ellingham. Bill Ellingham was introduced to me by Vicky Jim, the sister of my old schoolmate, Clifford. At that time, we were living in South Burnaby. Vicky and Bill had met and married after he divorced his first wife, Trudy. And Bill's story is too entertaining not to be included here.

Near the end of the Hungry Thirties, early in 1937, Bill Ellingham left his job as a dough maker in his father's Vancouver bakery and took a job as a ranch hand on a Cariboo cattle ranch. He had become bored with life in general in Vancouver and more specifically bored with working in a bakery. He thought he needed something more exciting.

Working as a ranch hand was certainly a healthy life out in the fresh air, and it was a big change from working inside a bakery and making bread dough day in and day out. And then, too, working with a crew of ranch hands wasn't a bit lonely as it often was in the bakery.

Now, out in the world, Bill was doing okay. He was single, debt free, and he had been able to save around $550. Most of his fellow workers spent their money as fast as they made it on wine, women, and song — or more aptly on beer, girls, and fancy cowboy apparel.

But, truth be told, Bill was becoming bored with being a cowboy too — bored with rounding up cattle on the range, working out in the weather, and driving the herd to the nearest railroad station at the end of the summer and loading it into CPR cattle cars. (From there, the cattle were taken to Vancouver, then slaughtered and sold as beef.)

Bill had heard of a small bakery for sale in the town of Lillooet. The price was four hundred dollars. He could afford that and still have money left over for start-up expenses. So in 1938 he quit his job as a ranch hand and journeyed to Lillooet, where he looked up the owner of the bakery. Bill scanned the property: a lot in the middle of town, and a house remodelled to accommodate a bakery oven and a show room. He was pleased by the compact apple orchard in the front yard, but most of all, he was pleased with the layout of the bakery, its location on Main Street, and especially the good condition of the oven.

Bill bought the property for four hundred dollars, and the Ellingham Lillooet Bakery was born.

After a week of cleaning out the premises, ordering supplies, and calling on the local stores to see who would be willing to become customers, Bill decided to spend the weekend socializing with the town folk, introducing himself, and dropping into the legion pub for a beer.

Before long, he learned that the local dance orchestra was

losing its pianist, so he jumped right in and arranged to meet the orchestra leader, Ken Pritchard. He told Ken that he was a trained pianist. They went to the community hall, where Bill demonstrated his piano skills. Ken was impressed! Bill easily played several popular pieces by ear, and quite as easily sight-read from the sheet music the leader had brought along. As a child, Bill had studied piano and was really a skilled musician.

He was welcomed with open arms. Socially, he told himself, things were looking up!

Within a week, Bill was in business, baking bread. Two of the three stores quickly signed up as customers, and the holdout, Cordelle's Cash and Carry, was persuaded by Curtis Lang, an old friend of Bill's, to sign up with Bill—or else! Curtis, as head of a logging crew, bought all his supplies from Cordelle, and he threatened to go elsewhere if Cordelle didn't buy Bill's bread.

Over the next two months, Bill's business grew, and he started baking cakes, pies, and cookies, and frying doughnuts. People were glad, too, to have him playing piano for the Saturday night dances. He quickly became a popular figure in the small town. He was even given a piano by Ma Murray, owner of the *Bridge River Lillooet News* and the Gold Nugget movie theatre.

"That piano is not being used in the theater," Ma said, "and you need a piano, so you can have it to play on at home." He couldn't have been more pleased: a piano, a gift from Ma Murray!

Bill soon needed help with bread deliveries, so he hired a high school student, fourteen-year-old George Donaghy, to push the bicycle-wheeled cart, loaded with wrapped bread, from store to store. Bill told me years later that George was obviously malnourished, so when he arrived after school, Bill's first wife Trudy fed him tea and sandwiches.

Business prospered until World War II broke out in Europe. Then Bill started to suffer from wartime shortages, especially of one item: lard. Lard was essential for bread making but also for deep-frying doughnuts, one of Bill's most popular specialties. He had to make a difficult decision: he stopped making doughnuts. He explained to his disappointed customers, "Lard is rationed because of the war."

People dropped by the bakery to complain. "When are you going to start making doughnuts again, Bill? We sure miss those delicious, fresh doughnuts."

"Well," Bill explained, over and over, "Lard is rationed, butter is rationed! It's the war! I am allowed only so much lard per month, and most of it has to go into my bread production. Doughnut making—deep-frying—uses a lot of lard, which I can't get from my supplier, Burns Company, in Vancouver. So there it is. No lard, no doughnuts. Sorry!"

One of Bill's most devoted customers was a Swede by the name of Gus Strom, who lived in a log cabin on the outskirts of town. One day, Gus came through the screen door, stepped up to the sales counter, and rang the little silver bell to announce his presence.

Bill's wife Trudy greeted him. "Good morning, Mr. Strom. How are you today?"

"I'm yoost fine," replied Gus in his Swedish accent, "but I sure miss dose doughnuts. Ven is Bill gonna make some more doughnuts?"

"Just a minute," said Trudy. "I'll get Bill." She disappeared into the back of the bakery.

Bill appeared. "Good morning, Gus. What's up?"

Gus replied sadly, "Ven you gonna start makin' more doughnuts, Bill?"

Bill very slowly explained to Gus that he was between a rock and a hard place when it came to lard, or anything at all in which to fry his coveted doughnuts.

"Look, Bill," Gus said excitedly. "I can get you lots of cooking oil. Should be good for frying doughnuts. I got two gallons in my cabin right now."

"Can you bring me some this afternoon?" said Bill.

"Yeah, sure. I will go home now and bring it to you," Gus replied, with a grin a mile wide.

Well, Gus trotted off, and in an hour he was back, out of breath, with a gallon of mineral oil in each hand. He handed the two gallons to Bill, who said, "I wonder. Is it really safe to deep-fry doughnuts in mineral oil?"

"I use it all the time to fry my eggs," Gus immediately retorted. "I fry potatoes, and I fry onions, chicken, bannock bread. I fry evert'ng, and I'm okay. Take a look at me." And Gus stood up and stuck his chest out, a big smile on his face.

"Okay," Bill said. "I'll give it a try."

So, next morning, when Gus appeared at the bakery, he was happy to see a pile of doughnuts on the counter, hidden behind a pile of fresh bread. Bill handed him a dozen doughnuts in a brown paper bag. "Here you are, Gus. Take them home and try them."

Next morning, Gus appeared at the bakery, smiling, and ordered his usual dozen to take home. Bill asked him how he felt, and Gus said, "I'm in better shape than I was yesterday."

"Well," said Bill, "they must be okay, then. I'll make doughnuts tomorrow morning after the bread is in the oven."

Gus spread the word, and next morning, a rush of doughnut lovers arrived at the bakery to make their orders.

That was on Tuesday.

By Friday, doughnut lovers were complaining of stomach cramps and IBS: irritable bowel syndrome. Actually, they all had diarrhea, and the culprit, according to Dr. Ployart, was the mineral oil Bill was using to deep-fry his doughnuts.

Word spread rapidly, and after three days, Bill's doughnut sales hit rock bottom. But worse than that, the town was quickly running out of toilet paper. Even Ma Murray's *Bridge River Lillooet News* had been used up. You might say the town of Lillooet was scraping the bottom of their paper supply.

Ma Murray was indignant. "Why don't they use their Eaton's catalogues?"

One of Ma Murray's political enemies, a CCFer—a member of the Co-operative Commonwealth Federation party —joyfully remarked, "You might as well wipe your ass on Ma Murray's bloody Liberal newspaper. That's all it's good for, anyway!"

Bill was dismayed and publicly apologetic, but he said to anyone who was within earshot, "I'm only partly to blame. Gus Strom ate the same doughnuts, and he never once got diarrhea! How in hell was I to know that, over the years, Gus had built up a resistance to mineral oil?"

Well, a month passed. People kept saying that they didn't blame Bill, and they secretly hoped that Bill could somehow convince someone on the ration board in Victoria to make an exception for doughnut frying. But Bill knew the writing was on the wall.

And then a miracle happened!

Joe Callum, the Burns Company salesman, came twice a month to Lillooet to deliver supplies to Bill's bakery. This day, when he had finished his delivery, Trudy happened to come in from the post office with their mail, and she invited Joe to stay and have coffee with her and Bill. Joe was more than happy to sit and enjoy the local gossip. Besides, Bill made really delicious oatmeal cookies, Joe's favourite treat.

As they sat and chatted in the living room, Joe suddenly spotted the piano. His eyes lit up. "Which one of you plays the piano?"

"Bill is a wonderful pianist," said Trudy. "He plays in the Lillooet dance orchestra."

Joe didn't hesitate. "Bill would you mind playing the piano for me right now, if you have the time?"

"Of course not," said Bill. "You sit and finish your coffee, and I'll play some dance tunes for you."

Joe sat, entranced, while Bill played several popular pieces.

Then Bill played short student pieces he had learned as a child. Finally, he turned to Joe. "I was lucky, Joe. My parents knew I was musical, and more important, they somehow knew that I wanted to play an instrument. So one day they asked me which instrument, and I answered, 'Piano.' That's how I got to I study piano and learn to play popular music, the music I love. The piano and Trudy are the two greatest loves of my life."

"God," Joe said, "I wish I had taken piano lessons as a child."

"Well, Joe, why not start now? I'll be your teacher. You will have to get yourself a piano to practise on in Vancouver. I can give you a lesson every two weeks, and I bet you in six months, you will be able to read music and play a lot of easy pieces."

"We have a piano in our home in Vancouver," Joe said. "My wife has had lessons and used to play, but she has lost interest, and now the piano just sits there."

"Let's start your first lesson right now," said Bill, "if you have an hour to spare."

"I have plenty of time today," said Joe.

So Bill rummaged around and found a beginner's piano instruction book. "Come on, Joe. Sit down at the piano. You can keep this book, take it home, practise what I'll teach you today, and come back in two weeks for your second lesson."

"Wow," exclaimed Joe excitedly. "How much do you want for each lesson?"

"Well," said Bill, almost in a whisper, "I'd like to make a deal with you, Joe. I don't want money. I want lard. You can pay me with so much lard per lesson — under the table, of course. Nobody has to know. Okay? How much lard can you get me?"

"I'll get you all the lard you want," whispered Joe. "I've got extra lard right now, outside in my van."

Bill was back in doughnut production. George Donaghy, Bill's bread-delivery boy, spread the gospel the next day on his rounds. All Bill's old customers flocked back to the bakery for free samples. Even Gus Strom showed up, unashamedly mixing with the crowd.

Bill pulled Gus to one side. "Well, Gus, what do think of these real lard doughnuts?"

"Dese lard doughnuts, Bill, are really good—but dose mineral oil doughnuts vas one helluva lot of fun!"

Homeward to the Cariboo - An Elegy

Benches of grey sand under sombre clay bluffs
for memory to sit sad upon
and see itself

Trudging in tennis shoes toe-holed and worn
clumping along flats barren and burned drying
in the sun's glare among prickly pear cactus that
rejoices as sagebrush and loneliness mourn the
hot July sun

Huddling under tall green ponderosa pine trees
blistering in the rays of a July mud wasp sun and
pausing to gaze on a backwash of boulders at
pine needles twisting old memory's wounds and
conjuring up flashes of an extraordinary ordinary
bright blue sky

A boy had the power to love such a land to
savour sweetness where others find salt and
know again strange things buried in the past
old mysteries and young dreams gleaming on a
jackknife blade.

A pair of deft hands pressing the sharp edges
of a lifetime together sharp fingered but unbled
in the aliveness, in the nearness and the now
as one grows old and multiplies while others
drain their eyes

Memory freshens and dries tearful eyes and old
sadness slips away letting beauty return to see
black cap, chokecherry, soopallalies bloom again

flinging their silent sweetness into eyes that sit
huddled under hills that crumble like the chalk
of old bones.

And below, the Fraser serpentines and unwinds
and twines a greyness that splits the house in two,
half-dead yet alive with the corpse of cows and boys
and cowboy Indians in July, riding their pink silk
yellow, blue, red and green bandanas up and down
the streets of the vanished
horseback town.

ACKNOWLEDGMENTS

I would like to express my appreciation to my daughters, Kathy and Laurel, for encouraging me to finally write these stories down. I also want to thank my good friends Paul Bjarnason and Nadia Romanovskaya. I thank Paul for his constant encouragement and support; he is always willing to read my poems and stories, and I welcome his valuable suggestions and constructive criticism. Nadia has also encouraged me to keep writing and has helped me lay out my poems. My daughter Laurel coordinated the effort to get the stories published with the help of a small, talented team of coaches. In particular, I wish to thank Amanda Bidnall for her editorial work; Laurel and I both learned a great deal from her. Finally, I want to thank my wife's sister Diane VanDyke for reading the entire manuscript and for her help with the editing.

ABOUT THE AUTHOR

Gordon E. Whitney was born in 1925 in Lillooet, BC, the town known as "mile zero" of the Gold Rush trail and the setting for the stories in this collection. Gordon's family moved away from Lillooet in 1939, when he was fourteen, and he completed high school in New Westminster. Gordon graduated from UBC in 1947 with a degree in geological engineering, but after three years in the Alberta oil fields, he returned to Vancouver and attended the Provincial Normal School from 1950 to 1951, graduating with honours as a high school mathematics teacher. In 1951, he began a thirty-four-year teaching career at Gladstone Secondary School. During those years, he sponsored the Gladstone Poetry Club, which published *The Juggler*, Gladstone's annual poetry magazine.

He met Joanne Reynolds while attending Normal School in 1950, and they were married in 1954. They purchased a lot in south Burnaby, where they built a home and raised their four children. Their family vacations frequently included visits with the "old-timers" in Lillooet and fishing excursions on Cayoosh Creek.

After Gordon retired from teaching, he completed a diploma in fine arts at Langara College, winning the award for top student. His hobbies include playing guitar and ukulele, drawing and painting, learning foreign languages, writing poetry, gardening, and fishing. Gordon will celebrate his ninety-fifth birthday in December 2020.

MORE FROM THE AUTHOR

Gordon E. Whitney lives in south Burnaby. He welcomes suggestions, questions and comments from readers about the characters and events he describes in his "Lillooet Stories."

Find him at: gewhitney.com

His other stories, poems and artwork are also available on this site.